FELLOW W   ɪH GOD

☷ Foundations series

Testifying to the faith and creativity of the Orthodox Christian
Church, the Foundations series draws upon the riches of its
tradition to address the modern world. These survey texts are
suitable both for preliminary inquiry and deeper investigation,
in the classroom and for personal study.

Peter C. Bouteneff
Series Editor

BOOK 5 OF THE FOUNDATIONS SERIES

Fellow Workers with God

ORTHODOX THINKING ON THEOSIS

Norman Russell

ST VLADIMIR'S SEMINARY PRESS
CRESTWOOD, NEW YORK
2009

Library of Congress Cataloging-in-Publication Data

Russell, Norman, 1945–
    Fellow workers with God : Orthodox thinking on theosis / by Norman Russell.
        p. cm. — (Foundations series bk. 5)
    Includes bibliographical references and index.
    ISBN 978–0–88141–339–7
        1. Deification (Christianity).   2. Orthodox Eastern Church—
Doctrines. I. Title.

BT767.8.R88 2009
234—dc22

                                                                  2009014342

© 2009 BY NORMAN RUSSELL

ST VLADIMIR'S SEMINARY PRESS
575 Scarsdale Rd, Yonkers, NY 10707
1–800–204–2665
www.svspress.com

ISSN 1556–9837
ISBN 978–0–88141–339–7

PRINTED IN THE UNITED STATES OF AMERICA

"We are God's fellow workers."
1 Corinthians 3.9

CONTENTS

foreword

From relative obscurity, "theosis" has in recent decades become a buzzword in Orthodox Christianity. In fact it has become something of an emblem. In the ecumenical context, people invoke theosis in order to give a nod to Orthodox understandings of salvation. Some also see it as an Orthodox antidote to the overly transactional understanding of atonement that is sometimes found in the Christian West.

Among professional and amateur theologians alike, the word theosis can be heard everywhere. But as is the case for many ubiquitous theological terms, few people are prepared to explain or even to understand what it means or what it might imply for our lives as we live them.

I have long been aware of this problem. While a seminarian in the late 1980s, I was sitting at lunch with Bishop Seraphim Sigrist, who was later to become a good friend. Like many of my peers, I was rattling on about theosis. And he asked, "Yes, well what is it?"

I tried to respond: "Well, deification." "Becoming as God is." "Participation in divine nature." These were rote answers, to which he kept firing back, "Yes, but what is it?" Not "What does it mean?" but "What *is* it?"

I could not answer to the satisfaction of either of us, and I don't think that this paralysis was unique to me.

Fortunately, the past two decades have seen several important books and conferences on theosis that have gone a long way to help. But the persistent memory of that conversation, added to my more recent, feeble attempts to speak about theosis in the classroom, led me to elicit a Foundations Series book that would bring ancient and modern voices together in conversation, with the goal of presenting a coherent understanding in accessible language. The search for such a study has taken four years. Some excellent theologians produced strong material during that time but each project ultimately fell through. Then Norman Russell mentioned to me his interest in producing an accessible book on the subject. Knowing him as the author of a magisterial academic study on theosis,[1] I was full of joyous expectations, all of which have been utterly exceeded by the present book.

One of this book's benefits lies in its treatment of the sources. Russell constantly refers to the Church Fathers as his authorities, but rather than paraphrasing them, he lets them speak directly. And when they disagree, he does not force unison nor does he leave the reader stuck in ambiguity, but identifies their agreement on fundamental tenets. He also lets modern Orthodox voices speak, giving the same respect to their convergences and divergences, deftly finding harmony among the various voices. He has thoroughly read not only the voluminous and sometimes abstruse work of twentieth-century philosophers and theologians Nikolai Berdyaev, Sergius Bulgakov, and Vladimir Lossky, but also that of more recent thinkers such as Christos Yannaras (much of whose work Russell himself has translated into English) and John Zizioulas, as well as contemporary Orthodox and Lutheran authors.

[1] *The Doctrine of Deification in the Greek Patristic Tradition* (Oxford University Press, 2004).

Some of the themes we encounter frequently in these pages will be familiar to scholars of theology, though they may be new to more casual readers: the essence/energies distinction, ekstasis and eros, and "personalism" (the idea that personhood, whether divine or human, is defined in terms of communion with the other). Russell's treatment makes each concept accessible to the non-specialist, while providing fresh insights for the more experienced. For example, he explores several dimensions of personalism as treated by various authors and their more recent critics. Along the way he also shows personalism to be a cornerstone of an Orthodox teaching on theosis: for theosis "expresses a *relation*, not a thing."

A feature that will make this book stand out, and make its readers especially grateful, is the author's ability to communicate the full depth and range of his knowledge of the subject in a way that is accessible and understandable. This should not be taken for granted, for as many authors (and their bemused readers) know, it is rare that a specialist cares enough to rethink his or her subject in non-specialist terms. Russell has taken the time to translate his scholarly approach into clear writing for a lay audience, casting aside the mantle of prestige to address people where they actually are.

I cannot imagine a more reliable or a more approachable cross-section of this vital aspect of ancient and contemporary Orthodox thought. It will no longer be possible to use "theosis" in a way that is facile, "over-spiritualized," or abstract. We have now lost any excuse to do so.

—Peter Bouteneff

introduction
WHAT IS THEOSIS?

"In the Holy Scriptures, where God Himself speaks, we read of a unique call directed to us. God speaks to us human beings clearly and directly and He says: 'I said, "You are gods, sons of the Most High—all of you"' (Ps 81 (82).6 and Jn 10.34). Do we hear that voice? Do we understand the meaning of this calling? Do we accept that we should in fact be on a journey, a road which leads to Theosis? As human beings we each have this one, unique calling, to achieve Theosis." So wrote Archimandrite Christoforos Stavropoulos in the late 1960s.[1] Yet if you had asked the average Orthodox Christian only a decade earlier what theosis meant, you would probably have been met with a puzzled look. The word hardly featured in the standard theological handbooks.[2] It was a technical term familiar only to monks and patristic scholars. The change since that time has been remarkable: from relative obscurity, theosis has become a common expression summarizing the whole economy salvation.

---

[1] Stavropoulos, *Partakers of the Divine Nature* (Minneapolis, MN: Light and Life, 1976), 17.

[2] For example, in Trembelas's massive three-volume *Dogmatics* (Athens, 1959–1961), theosis is confined to a brief mention in the final pages of the last volume.

What happened to bring about this change? There were four crucial factors: the rediscovery of the teaching of St Gregory Palamas, the impact of Russian religious philosophy, the recovery of the spirituality of the *Philokalia*, and the reengagement of Orthodox scholars with the early Greek Fathers. The key factor, perhaps, was the rediscovery of the teaching of St Gregory Palamas.[3] This was occasioned by the publication in 1931 of an article on St Gregory by Martin Jugie in the authoritative *Dictionnaire de théologie catholique*.[4] Jugie, a member of an Augustinian religious congregation and a great expert on Byzantine theology, declared Palamas's distinction between the essence and the energies of God to be fundamentally wrong and his notion of deifying uncreated grace to be "near to heresy."[5] This provoked a vigorous response from the Russian community which had established itself in Paris after the Bolshevik revolution of 1917 and Lenin's expulsion of prominent intellectuals in 1922. Their defense of Palamas soon led to an exposition of theosis, which was perceived to rest primarily on the essence-energies distinction. If this debate had been conducted in Russian it would have attracted relatively little attention. The fact that it was conducted in French was to have far-reaching consequences.

[3]Jeffrey D. Finch, "Neo-Palamism, Divinizing Grace, and the Breach between East and West," in *Partakers of the Divine Nature* (ed. Michael J. Christensen and Jeffery A. Wittung: Madison/Teaneck: Fairleigh Dickinson University Press, 2007), 233–249. (Date of Jugie's article corrected.)

[4]"Palamas Grégoire," *Dictionnaire de théologie catholique* 11. 1735–76.

[5]Ibid., 1764.

The Contribution of the Russians

The first books written and published in Paris by the exiled Russian scholars were in their native language. Titles in French only began to appear in the 1930s. One of the earliest of these was a series of articles on the doctrine of deification to the end of the eleventh century by Myrrha Lot-Borodine (1882–1957), published in 1932–1933. Next came Vladimir Lossky's (1903–1958) brilliant *Mystical Theology of the Eastern Church*, originally published in 1944, which defined "union with God or deification, the *theosis* of the Greek Fathers," as the goal of the Christian life. Finally, in 1959, came John Meyendorff's landmark work, *A Study of Gregory Palamas*, which presented theosis as the crowning achievement of St Gregory's spiritual teaching.

The cumulative effect of these French-language works on non-Orthodox and Orthodox alike was sensational. Some Western Christians expressed hostility but many were delighted to discover a dimension of Orthodox spiritual life previously unknown to them. The French Jesuit—later Cardinal—Jean Daniélou later wrote of his excitement at coming across in Lot-Borodine's work what he had unconsciously been seeking for a long time, "a vision of humanity transfigured by the divine energies."[6] The effect on Orthodox readers was hardly less dramatic. When the Greek edition of Lossky's book was published in 1964, it was immediately a bestseller. Indeed, a Greek theological renaissance was set in motion in the 1960s largely as a result of this book. In Thessalonica a whole school of Palamite studies developed, resulting in the main works of St Gregory being published for the first time.

[6]Myrrha Lot-Borodine, *La Déification de l'homme selon la doctrine des Pères grecs* (Paris: Éditions du Cerf, 1970), 10.

Important studies of Palamite thought also appeared, such as
Georgios Mantzaridis, *Palamika* (1973), translated into English
as *The Deification of Man* (1984).

Parallel to this resurgence of interest in St Gregory Palamas there
was also a growing influence of Russian religious philosophy. This
was a philosophical tradition quite different from that of the West,
which since the seventeenth century has been accustomed to making a sharp distinction between philosophy and theology. When
serious philosophical thought began in Russia in the nineteenth
century, it was taken for granted that any investigation into the
nature of reality must also take account of its religious dimension.
One of the most important works of religious philosophy in this
period was Vladimir Solovyev's *Lectures on Godmanhood* (based
on lectures given in 1878–1881). Solovyev (1853–1900) was pro-
foundly aware of the fragmented nature of the human being. Our
greatest need, he was convinced, is to return to our original unity.
We can do this only through Christ's mystical body in which
divinity and humanity are perfectly united. For us to share in
Christ the God-man, and thus come to participate in the divine
life, there must be some divine element already within us which
makes this possible. The purpose of the Christian life is to nurture
this element. Solovyev's spiritual heirs, particularly S. L. Frank
(1877–1950) and Nicolas Berdyaev (1874–1948) popularized the
idea in a series of books translated into French in the 1930s and
1940s that we cannot attain our full stature as human beings
unless we realize our potentiality of union with God through
Christ, the supreme model of Godmanhood, or divine humanity.

The rediscovery of the *Philokalia*

Through these and the books previously mentioned, theosis began to regain a central position in the consciousness of Orthodox Christians as the context and goal of the Christian life. This was strengthened by another rediscovery: the spirituality of the *Philokalia*. The *Philokalia* is an anthology of spiritual texts, compiled by Makarios of Corinth and Nikodemos of the Holy Mountain from manuscripts preserved in the libraries of Mount Athos, which was published in Venice in 1782. Nikodemos reveals the intention underlying this work in the opening words of his preface:

> God, the blessed nature, perfection that is more than perfect, the creative principle of all that is good and beautiful, Himself transcending all goodness and all beauty, in His supremely divine plan preordained from all eternity the deification [*theosis*] of humankind.[7]

Lay people, Nikodemos hoped, would be encouraged to practice ceaseless prayer through the invocation of the Holy Name and so realize in their personal life the "supremely divine plan preordained from all eternity" for the human race as a whole, which is to partake of the very life of God.

In the difficult Byzantine Greek of the original these texts were not easily accessible. It was only when they came to be translated into modern languages that their full impact was felt. The first translation was into Russian (via Old Slavonic) made by the great nineteenth-century spiritual father, St Theophan the Recluse (1815–1894). Then came the Romanian version, translated by

---

[7]Quoted by Bishop Kallistos of Diokleia, "The Spirituality of the Philokalia," *Sobornost incorporating Eastern Churches Review* 13.1 (1991), 14.

one of the twentieth century's most distinguished Orthodox theologians, Father Dumitru Stăniloae (1903–1993). Selections in English began to appear in the 1950s. The enthusiastic reception of these encouraged the publishers to undertake the publication of the complete text, translated and edited by G.E.H. Palmer, Philip Sherrard and Kallistos Ware, the first volume of which appeared in 1979.

The *Philokalia* became well known in pre-revolutionary Russia, being reprinted four times between 1883 and 1913. It is no coincidence that it was Russian theologians who pioneered the Western world's recovery of a knowledge of theosis in the twentieth century. The books of Lossky and Meyendorff, together with renewed study of the *Philokalia*, led to the reappropriation of the Byzantine teaching on theosis by Orthodox theologians. Two of the best known, besides Father Stăniloae, are Professor Christos Yannaras and Metropolitan John Zizioulas. None of these writers treats theosis as a formal topic. But it permeates their thinking on the nature of the human person and the person's eschatological fulfillment at the final consummation of all things. The recovery of the notion of theosis has spread even beyond the bounds of the Orthodox communion. One of the most remarkable of these developments is the claim made by some Finnish Lutheran theologians that Luther himself accepted the idea of the deification of the Christian.[8] Under this influence work has been done recently

---

[8]These are theologians of the Finnish school of Luther research. See, for example, Tuomo Mannermaa, "*Theosis* as a subject of Finnish Luther Research," *Pro Ecclesia* 4 (1995), 37–48; Veli-Matti; Kärkkäinen, *One with God: Salvation as Deification and Justification*, (Collegeville, MN: Liturgical Press, 2004). Cf. the critique of the Finnish school's understanding of theosis in Gösta Hallonsten, "Theosis in Recent Research: A Renewal of Interest and a Need for Clarity." In Michael J. Christensen and Jeffery A. Wittung,

in the United States on various aspects of theosis in order to illuminate Protestant teaching on salvation.[9]

Theosis, from having once been an unfamiliar term, has now entered into common use. Yet its meaning is not as obvious as people sometimes assume. Consider the following statements by Orthodox theologians:

- "Deification must not remain a general spiritual category but must acquire a specific anthropological content, which in the language of the Fathers means a content at once anthropological and christological: that is to say, it must be understood again as Christification" (Panayiotis Nellas).[10]

- "Deification, then, has to do with human destiny, a destiny that finds its fulfillment in a face-to-face encounter with God, an encounter in which God takes the initiative

eds. *Partakers of the Divine Nature*. Madison/Teaneck: Fairleigh Dickinson University Press, 2007, 281–293.

[9]Recent conferences which have generated collective publications include "Consultation on Orthodox and Wesleyan Spirituality," held at St Vladimir's Orthodox Seminary in 2001, resulting in S. T. Kimbrough Jr, ed., *Orthodox and Wesleyan Spirituality* (Crestwood, NY: St Vladimir's Seminary Press, 2002); and "Partakers of the Divine Nature," held at Drew University in 2004, resulting in Stephen Finlan and Vladimir Kharlamov, eds., *Theōsis: Deification in Christian Theology* (Eugene, OR: Pickwick Publications, 2006), and Michael J. Christensen and Jeffery A. Wittung, eds., *Partakers of the Divine Nature: The History and Development of Deification in the Christian Traditions* (Madison/Teaneck: Fairleigh Dickinson University Press, 2007).

[10]Panayiotis Nellas, *Deification in Christ: Orthodox Perspectives on the Nature of the Human Person*, trans. Norman Russell (Crestwood, NY: St Vladimir's Seminary Press, 1987), 40.

by meeting us in the Incarnation, where we behold 'the glory as of the Only-Begotten from the Father' (Jn 1.14), 'the glory of God in the face of Jesus Christ' (2 Cor 4.6)" (Andrew Louth).[11]

- "Deification is God's perfect and full penetration of man. ... Deification in a broad sense begins at Baptism, and extends throughout the whole of man's spiritual ascent; here his powers are also active, that is, during the purification from passions, the attaining of the virtues, and illumination. In this ascent the natural powers of man are in continual growth, and reach their apogee once they become capable of seeing the divine light—the power of vision is the working of the Holy Spirit. Therefore we can say that the deification by which this revivification and growth is realized, coincides with the process of the development of human powers to their limit, or with the full realization of human nature, but also with their unending eclipse by grace. Deification never stops, but continues beyond the ultimate limits of the powers of human nature, to the infinite. The latter we can call deification in the strict sense" (Dumitru Stăniloae).[12]

- "For the person to be restored to his or her integrity and wholeness, for the human being to become 'all prosôpon'—'all person'—defines our existential end. It

---

[11]Andrew Louth, "The Place of *Theosis* in Orthodox Theology." In Michael J. Christensen and Jeffery A. Wittung, eds. *Partakers of the Divine Nature,* 34.

[12]Stăniloae, *Orthodox Spirituality* (South Canaan, PA: St Tikhon's Seminary Press, 2002), 362–63 (translation modified).

is the conclusion of our moral journey, the attainment of theosis or deification, the goal towards which the Church strives. . . ." (Christos Yannaras).[13]

Deification, or theosis, is a complex term with both anthropological and economic components—that is to say, it concerns our growth as human beings towards ultimate fulfilment in God, while simultaneously encompassing the whole of God's plan of salvation. In other words, it is both a theological theme and a spiritual teaching, both the *goal* of the divine economy and the *process* by which the economy is worked out in the believer. It is not surprising that it was several centuries before the Fathers were able to define the term. Even now it is not easy, but we need a working definition. One that uses elements from the four passages just quoted might run as follows: Theosis is our restoration as persons to integrity and wholeness by participation in Christ through the Holy Spirit, in a process which is initiated in this world through our life of ecclesial communion and moral striving and finds ultimate fulfillment in our union with the Father—all within the broad context of the divine economy. Complex as this definition sounds, all the elements (apart from the idea of union) were in place by the fourth century.

Theosis and the Fathers

The first to treat theosis as equivalent to union with God was the sixth-century Syrian writer who adopted as his pseudonym the name of St Paul's first convert in Athens, Dionysius the Areopagite. Dionysius gave us our first definition of theosis: "the attain-

[13]Christos Yannaras, *Person and Eros,* trans. Norman Russell (Brookline, MA: Holy Cross Orthodox Press, 2007), 293.

ing of likeness to God and union with him so far as possible"
(*Ecclesiastical Hierarchy* 1.3, 367A). But the word "theosis" is
older than that. It was created in the fourth century by St Gregory
of Nazianzus—he used it for the first time in 363 (*Oration* 4.71),
in a speech delivered shortly after the death of the Emperor Julian
the Apostate—to encapsulate a number of ideas, all relating to the
divine economy:

- The condescension of God in emptying himself to become
  incarnate;

- The taking up of the body he assumed into the divine
  life;

- The appropriation of this deified humanity by us at our
  baptism;

- The ascent of the human soul to God through the contemplative life;

- The fulfillment of our whole being in heaven.

Although he invented the term, Gregory of course did not invent the
ideas it signifies. The notion of theosis goes back to the second-century Fathers, Clement of Alexandria, Hippolytus of Rome and Irenaeus of Lyons, and even to the New Testament writers themselves
as they reflect on the significance of Christ in the Scriptures.

If we simply confine ourselves to Dionysius' definition, we shall
fail to appreciate the full scope of theosis—though even Dionysius' use of the term is more complex than might appear at first
sight. The second-century Fathers lived in a world in which ecclesiastical Christianity was in competition with other claimants to
truth. These were Christians who maintained they had privileged

access to esoteric apostolic traditions, or Jews who dismissed the Church's teaching about Christ as novel and unfounded, or pagans who took it for granted that the path to divine-human communion based on the study of the ancient philosophers was superior to any of its rivals.

Against pagans, Jews, and Gnostic Christians, the teachers of what we might call primitive orthodoxy taught that through Christ, as encountered in baptism and the Eucharist, human beings could attain a community of life with God in a manner which allowed them to be thought of as "gods." Sometimes the language could sound exotic—Clement of Alexandria speaks of the Christian deified by heavenly teaching who "becomes a god while still walking about in the flesh"—but in fact the idea of deification is rooted in the Church's interpretation of biblical texts.

In the second-century Fathers we find the idea of deification used in two fundamental ways: as a theological theme and as a teaching concerned with the spiritual life.

- As a theological theme it refers to the mystery of the Incarnation: "Because of his infinite love he became what we are in order to make us what he is himself."

- As a spiritual teaching it refers to our appropriation in and through Christ of the transformed humanity created by him: our task is to become "like God so far as possible."

The assertion that Christ "became what we are in order to make us what he is himself" belongs to Irenaeus of Lyons (*Against Heresies* 5, Preface). Athanasius rephrased it in the early fourth century, giving it what was to become its classic form: "He became human that we might become divine" (*On the Incarnation* 54). This we now call the "exchange formula." "He gave us divinity," as St Ephrem the Syrian puts it, "we gave him humanity" (*Hymns on Faith* 5.7). Expressed in this way, it is not obvious that the saying is the fruit of reflection on Scripture. But that is precisely what it is, based on Paul's claim that Christ "emptied himself, taking the form of a servant, being born in the likeness of men" and that after death on the Cross he was highly exalted by God and given the name which is above every name (Phil 2.5–11), taken in conjunction with two other statements: Paul's teaching that "you are the body of Christ" (1 Cor 12.27) and the verse from the Psalms: "I said, you are gods, and all of you sons of the Most High" (Ps 81.6). If those addressed by God are called "sons of the Most High," it is because they have become so through the adoption of baptism. And if the psalm verse makes these sons equivalent to "gods," it is because Christ has enabled believers to share in the divine life which he made incarnate. Through baptism and the Eucharist they participate in the body of Christ, the new humanity which Christ created and as a result of his Passion exalted to the highest heaven.

As a spiritual teaching theosis is still connected with the Incarnation, but under this heading it attempts to express what the Christian life is about in the language of the intellectual culture prevailing in the early centuries of the Christian era. That language, of course, was Greek. And contemporary philosophers, drawing on Plato (*Theaetetus* 176b), were saying that the purpose of a serious philosophical life was to become like God so far as possible. For the early Christians this resonated with the teaching of Genesis that humanity had been created in the image and likeness of God (Gen 1.26). The bringing together of Plato and

Moses, the assumed author of the book of Genesis, seemed quite natural in the second century in view of many people's conviction that Plato had borrowed his doctrines from Moses. Recovering the likeness lost as a result of the Fall was seen in terms of our becoming divine. The interpretation of biblical texts with the help of Plato was to have far-reaching consequences for the development of a theoretical framework for the spiritual life.

These two uses of deification, as a theological theme and as a spiritual teaching, did not remain in separate compartments. The thematic approach is closely connected with the sacramental life of the Church. As early as Irenaeus, although the term "theosis" was not yet available, the idea of deification was fully integrated into a theological vision of the truth about the human condition. According to Irenaeus, the Fall was not a human error that upset God's plans for us. Humankind was brought into being in order to be saved. We were in need of Christ from the beginning for the completion and fulfillment of our humanity. Christ's last word on the Cross *tetelestai*, ("it is finished," or better, "it is consummated") marks both the creation and the salvation of humanity. Thus through incorporation into Christ by baptism we share in the humanity endowed with divine life which he created. Baptism "mingles" us with the Word of God and enables us to become the dwelling-place of God. By being adopted as sons or daughters of God we are reunited with the source of life. We become the "gods" that Psalm 81 addresses.

Later writers take it for granted that the "gods" of the psalm are those whom God has adopted through baptism and continues to nourish through the Eucharist. This I would call the *realistic* approach to theosis. That is to say, while deification is still a metaphor, a poetic figure of speech, it expresses a real and intimate relationship with God. The way this relationship is achieved, as expressed in the ecclesial life of the Church, is through *participation*. By sharing in Christ sacramentally we can share in his attribute of divinity, which is eternal life with the Father.

Running parallel to this, theosis as a spiritual teaching is developed by those Fathers who offer guidance on the ascetic struggle to attain likeness to God. This I would call the *ethical* approach to theosis. It is the approach we find in the Cappadocian Fathers and many of the writers of the *Philokalia*. The separation of the will from the passions, the practice of ceaseless prayer, the return of the soul to its original beauty, the attainment of a final god-like perfection, may be the gift of divine grace but must be accompanied by moral effort. The way this relationship is achieved is through *imitation*, a striving to reflect God in our everyday life. Neither approach is independent of the other. The realistic needs the ethical, and the ethical the realistic. Participation and imitation go hand in hand. Theosis for the great fourth-century Fathers meant "putting on Christ," with all that that implied, the working out of our Christian vocation through participation in the sacramental life of the Church supported by the ascetic struggle to overcome the passions.

Historically, Orthodox thinking on theosis did not follow a smooth course. After Cyril of Alexandria (412–444) there was a gap. This was a result of the Christological controversies Cyril was caught up in. Against Nestorius, who spoke of two "persons" (by which he probably meant "roles") coming together in Christ to make a "personal" union by "conjunction," Cyril argued that Christ was a single "person" (which he understood in terms of *hypostasis*, or a subsistent entity) who had united himself with a human life that was complete in every respect, drawing it up into his divine being. Before the Nestorian crisis Cyril speaks of the deification of Christ's human nature, but later he abandons this, partly on account of Nestorius' caricaturing such deification as an "apotheosis" which swallows up Christ's human qualities. To avoid unnecessary criticism, Cyril resorts to a text largely ignored by the earlier Fathers: "partakers of the divine nature" (2 Pet 1.4). Using this text as a concise way of expressing how Christians can appropriate the divine life, he connects deification for the first time with the Trinity as a whole. When we partake of the divine nature we achieve a relationship with the Father through the Spirit in the Son.

Cyril's abandoning of the traditional vocabulary of deification led to its falling out of use for a century or more. It was reintroduced in a new format by Dionysius the Areopagite and Maximus the Confessor in the sixth century. For Dionysius theosis is the goal of participation in the body and blood of Christ, these being understood not in a corporeal fashion but intellectually as symbols elevating the mind to union with the divine attributes of goodness, oneness and deity. Maximus also focuses on the symbolic meaning of the Liturgy but with a greater emphasis on the Incarnation. The divine Word who created us also brought about our salvation by the mystery of the Passion. We participate in Christ through the deifying activity of the Spirit. Theosis is a grace given by the Spirit which enables us to imitate Christ, and ultimately share in his divine attributes of immortality, stability and immutability.

Theosis and hesychasm

Maximus reestablished theosis in a monastic context as the goal of the spiritual life. He also outlined the distinction between the essence and energies of God which Gregory Palamas was to make central to his own teaching on theosis. Until Palamas theosis was not a topic of discussion in the Byzantine Church because it was not controversial. This situation changed in the fourteenth century. In his sermons to the people of Thessalonica Palamas presents theosis in the style of Athanasius: the Word became incarnate "to turn human beings into sons of God and make them partakers of divine immortality" (*Hom.* 16). But in his dispute with the intellectuals on how human beings can participate in God, he develops St Maximus' distinction between the essence and the energies of God to suggest how we can share in the source of divine life without compromising God's utter transcendence. Theosis is experienced as participation in God as light, which is attainable even in this life by monks practicing the hesychast method of prayer.

Hesychasm was (and still is) a form of monastic life focused on the practice of the Jesus Prayer. Through the constant repetition of a brief invocation, in its full form: "Lord Jesus Christ, Son of God, have mercy on me, a sinner," the monk or nun seeks to still the chatter of the mind ("draw the mind into the heart") and consciously abide in the Holy Spirit, so that he or she, sharing in the life of Christ, is even granted on occasion a vision of immortal glory as a foretaste of the divine union to come.

Hesychasm spread from Mount Athos to Bulgaria and Romania and thence to Russia. This was the background against which the *Philokalia* was compiled. In Russia its teaching reached a broad public through an anonymous work, *The Way of a Pilgrim*, a deeply moving account of a simple Russian's search for God.

Theosis and modern Orthodox thought

Modern Orthodox thinking on theosis is to a large degree the fruit of this Russian experience. In the earlier part of the twentieth century Berdyaev in particular attracted a large readership with books on the human situation springing from a philosophy of personalism—the idea that the person is not a natural but an axiological category (i.e. a category to do with values), characterized above all by freedom of the spirit. Berdyaev's doctrine of personality was based on a theological view of humanity. He saw human beings not as fallen and sinful but as potentially exalted to heaven because God had become man. Hence "man is a being who surmounts and transcends himself."[14] The attaining of personhood consists in a perpetual transcending of the self, which reaches its fullest realization in an existential encounter with God.

In the middle of the twentieth century Lossky and Meyendorff, through their work on Gregory Palamas and the Church's mystical tradition, made the hesychast version of theosis widely known in the West and encouraged its revival in Orthodox countries such as Greece. In this they were assisted by Archbishop Basil Krivocheine (1900–1985), who pioneered the publication of texts by St Symeon the New Theologian. Meanwhile, in Romania, Stăniloae was engaged in translating and commenting on the *Philokalia*. In consequence, the Romanians, too, began to rediscover the teaching of the hesychast Fathers on union with God.

[14]Nicolas Berdyaev, *Slavery and Freedom*, trans. R. M. French (London: Geoffrey Bles, 1943), 29.

Finally, the earlier patristic tradition that preceded the hesychasts was recovered in the second half of the twentieth century. Here the stimulus was provided by Western scholars, particularly those who led the post-war revival of patristic studies that resulted, among other things, in the founding of the *Sources chrétiennes* series of patristic texts with facing French translations. In Greece a series inspired by *Sources chrétiennes*, called *Epi tas Pēgas* ("Back to the Sources") was launched in 1968 by Panayiotis Nellas (1936–1986), whose own studies resulted in 1979 in a volume on theosis published in English under the title *Deification in Christ* (1987).

Recent Orthodox thinking on theosis thus draws on three main sources: modern personalist philosophy, fourteenth-century hesychast doctrine, and the teaching of the early Greek Fathers. In the following chapters, as we consider different thinkers in some detail, we shall see how varied they are in their emphasis. "Varied" in this context does not imply incompatibility, any more than it does in the Fathers themselves. In my discussion I shall be forthright about the disagreements of modern Orthodox scholars, but I hope to show with equal clarity that their views are fundamentally convergent.

The logic of this book

In keeping with the idea of unity-in-diversity, in this book I approach theosis from a number of different angles. The seven chapters fall into two groups, the first four more biblical and theological in their emphasis, the last three more speculative. They invite us to take part in a journey. In the first group we begin with the broad scope of the divine economy (Ch. 1), and then narrow our angle of vision as we work through specific texts and themes to do with important aspects of the economy (Chs. 2 and 3), until we arrive at the apostolic vision that encapsulates the whole of the economy in a single scene—Christ transfigured on Mount Tabor between Moses and Elijah (Ch. 4). In the second group of chapters our angle of vision widens again as we ascend from self-transcendence (Ch. 5) to participation in the divine energies (Ch. 6) and ultimately to union with God (Ch. 7). (Would that it were so!) In the Epilogue I shall take stock and assess what Orthodox thinkers have contributed to our understanding of our unique calling as human beings to achieve theosis.

chapter one
THEOSIS AND THE
ECONOMY OF SALVATION

The meaning of the divine economy

W hen we speak of the divine economy we mean God's saving plan for the human race. The divine economy, realized in the incarnate Son, enables us to become partakers of the divine nature, to be fulfilled as human beings transformed by the power of God.

This summary statement needs unpacking. "Economy" (in Greek, *oikonomia*) originally meant "household management." It was later used as a metaphor for any organization or dispensation of human affairs. The expression "divine economy," first used by Clement of Alexandria in the second century, represents a further extension of the senses of "organization" and "dispensation" to take in the story of God's dealings with humankind. This gives rise to a number of questions. In what way does the history of divine-human relations as a sequence of events reflect the reality of a God who is beyond time? More generally, what does the Incarnation tell us about the nature of God? The older style of dogmatic handbooks began by considering God in his oneness and threeness—the "Triune God"—and then proceeded to discuss how one of the Trinity became incarnate. God "in himself" (though from what standpoint we could take a detached view of God's inner life was never made clear) was called the "immanent" Trinity. The "economic Trinity" was then the manifestation of God's activity as recorded in the Scriptures. The "divine economy" was therefore the story of God's dealings with humanity in terms of a historical progression from creation via the Fall to redemption in Christ. The problem with this approach, as Father John Behr has pointed out in *The Mystery of Christ* (2006), is that it tends to put the truth about Jesus firmly in the past. The life and work of Christ become an episode in history which may be analyzed like any other. As a result, much recent discussion about "who Jesus really was" is actually no more than our own reconstruction of the past on the basis of modern criteria of historical plausibility.

This can be very interesting. Modern research has unearthed much fascinating information about conditions in first-century Palestine. But the idea that we can recapture the "historical Jesus" by filtering out the "Jesus of faith" is illusory. Neither philosophical deduction from first principles nor historical reconstruction from the literary and archaeological sources can answer the question put to disciples and hence to us: "Who do you say that I am?" What we need to do in order to respond to the question is to follow the first disciples, for they came to understand Christ only in the light of the Passion when they turned to the Scriptures as a storehouse of images illuminating his true significance. The Scriptures, of course, were the Old Testament—the New had yet to be written. It was there that the truth about Jesus was to be found. What unlocked this truth, as Father Behr has recently reminded us, was the Passion as the focal point of the revelation of God's transformative power.

Before the Passion the disciples may have lived in daily intimacy with Jesus, but their understanding was nevertheless limited. It was only after the Passion that they understood the truth. And the truth was that in Jesus Christ we can, through the Spirit, know the Father. To see Christ is to know what it means to be God. In more technical language, the Word of God made flesh is the "place" where God's self-expression is made accessible to us through the divine Spirit. "God was in Christ," as St Paul says, "reconciling the world to himself" (2 Cor 5.19). But the truth is not only known by looking back into the past. The early Christians looked forward to the exalted Christ, to the "coming one" who was to consummate gloriously and publicly the divine reconciliation achieved by his Passion and Resurrection.

The divine economy encompasses the reconciliation and glorification of humankind through Christ. This is not the fruit of an act of the omnipotent divine will but requires our cooperation and response in faith. For we participate in the divine economy by embodying God's presence in the world through our own Christian witness. Or, as Mother Maria of Normanby has put it:

> Because Christ is perfect Love, his life on earth can never become a life of the past. He remains present to all eternity. Then he was alone, and bore the sins of men as one whole, alone. But, in death, he took us all into his work. Therefore the Gospel is now present with us. We may enter inside his own sacrifice.[1]

Embodying the presence of God, participating in the work of reconciliation, entering into Christ's sacrifice–these lie at the heart of

[1]Quoted by Kallistos Ware, *The Orthodox Way* (Crestwood, NY: St Vladimir's Seminary Press, 1979), 115.

the meaning of theosis and are summed up in the phrase from St Peter's second letter, "partakers of the divine nature" (2 Pet 1.4). As Christians transformed by Christ we become not "who" God is but "what" he is, sharing in his divine plan for the reconciliation and glorification of humankind.

The vocabulary of deification

All theological language is rooted in metaphor. Redemption, for example, means literally "being ransomed or bought back." Salvation means "being made safe and whole." Theosis, or "becoming god," implies more than redemption or salvation. It is not simply the remedying of our defective human state. It is nothing less than our entering into partnership with God, our becoming fellow workers with him (1 Cor 3.9) for the sake of bringing the divine economy to its ultimate fulfillment.

The actual words the Fathers use to express this are worth exploring. "Theosis," formed from the verb *theoō*, "to make god," was the term that became established in the Byzantine Church after the seventh century as a result of its use by Gregory of Nazianzus, Dionysius the Areopagite and Maximus the Confessor. But earlier, a broader vocabulary was used. In the second century Irenaeus of Lyons speaks of the baptized becoming "gods". Clement of Alexandria, a younger contemporary of Irenaeus, uses the verbs "to deify" (*theopoieō*) and "to apotheosize" (*apotheoō*), and Origen, the great Alexandrian theologian of the following generation, does the same. In the fourth century St Athanasius, also of Alexandria, speaks several times of the "deification" (*theopoiēsis*) of the Christian.

Remarkably, although none of these terms was used by any biblical author, the Fathers who introduced them did so without any apparent reservation. They did not even see any need for explanation. The terms did not sound crypto-pagan to them, as they might to a modern ear, or even particularly exotic. Certainly, they were sometimes used with reference to pagan deification, but in fact they had already become secularized in everyday usage, at least amongst intellectuals. This was largely due to an Alexandrian scholar called Euhemerus, who was one of the first rationalizing historians of ancient religion. It was his theory that the classical gods had all been human at some stage and had been awarded divine honors because of the power they had exercised or the benefactions they had conferred on their subjects or fellow citizens. Deification was thus associated with the acquisition of virtue through noble conduct. It was easy for Christians to appropriate the terms without taking over their pagan content.

By the fourth century a distinctive Christian vocabulary had begun to emerge. Christians used the nouns *theopoiēsis* and *theōsis*, and the correlative verbs *theopoieō* and *theoō*. In the meantime some Greek philosophers, mainly Neoplatonists, were beginning to use the language of theosis. But in their case they adopted a slightly different set of terms, preferring the noun *ektheōsis* and the verb *ektheoō*, meaning "to make fully divine." They used these to refer to a characteristically Neoplatonic idea: the effect of a divine power reaching downwards through the hierarchy of being from the source of divinity, the One, with the intention of drawing up all beings endowed with mind into unity with itself. This notion was to have considerable influence on Christian thought, but not until the sixth century, when it was adapted to Christian use by Dionysius the Areopagite. Even though we find some parallels to

Christian deification in pagan writers, it was thus Christians who led the way.

The place of theosis in the divine economy

The vocabulary of theosis was developed to express a spiritual teaching concerning our appropriation through Christ of the humanity that was transformed by him as a result of his Incarnation, Passion and Resurrection. Some modern writers have adopted the idea of theosis in isolation from Christian theology as a term descriptive of a program for developing the transcendent aspect of the self. But this is not how Orthodoxy sees it. Theosis is not a piece of what we might call theological "bricolage" to be added to a personally constructed set of beliefs.[2] It has a structural significance that determines our whole understanding of salvation and the conduct which ought to flow from it. The Fathers expressed this in what has come to be known as the "exchange formula."[3] Here are some of their statements:

- The Son of God "became what we are in order to make us what he is himself" (Irenaeus, *Against Heresies* 5, pref.).

[2]I have borrowed the term "bricolage" (French for "do it yourself" hardware) from Fr Gabriel Rochelle, "Apophatic Preaching and the Postmodern Mind," *SVTQ* 50 (2006), 397–419.

[3]Referred to sometimes in Latin as the *admirabile commercium*. Gösta Hallonsten has made the interesting observation that the *admirabile commercium* has remained simply a "theological theme" in the West, while in the East it expresses "a comprehensive doctrine that encompasses the whole of the economy of salvation." Therefore "A real *doctrine of theosis* . . . is to be found only in the East" ("*Theosis* in Recent Research," 287; 292).

- "The Word of God became man so that you too may learn from a man how it is even possible for a man to become a god" (Clement of Alexandria, *Exhortation to the Greeks* 1.8.4).

- "He became human that we might become divine" (Athanasius, *On the Incarnation* 54).

- "He gave us divinity, we gave him humanity" (Ephrem, *Hymns on Faith* 5.7).

- "Let us become as Christ is, since Christ became as we are; let us become gods for his sake, since he became man for our sake" (Gregory of Nazianzus, *Oration* 1.5).

- The Word became incarnate "so that by becoming as we are, he might make us as he is" (Gregory of Nyssa, *Refutations* 11).

- "The Son of God became the Son of Man that he might make the sons of men sons of God" (Augustine, *Mainz sermons* 13.1).

- "He became like us, that is, a human being, that we might become like him, I mean gods and sons. On the one hand he accepts what belongs to us, taking it to himself as his own, and on the other he gives us in exchange what belongs to him" (Cyril of Alexandria, *Commentary on John* 12.1).

- "God and man are paradigms of one another, that as much as God is humanized to man through love for mankind, so much has man been able to deify himself to God through love" (Maximus the Confessor, *Ambigua* 10).

From Irenaeus in the second century to Maximus in the seventh many of the Fathers see theosis as summarizing the very purpose of the Incarnation—the loving self-emptying of God (kenosis) evoking a fervent human response (theosis), the divinization of the human person mirroring the humanization of the divine Word. The relationship is reciprocal but not entirely symmetrical. Even in the person of Christ the human and the divine both give and receive. But the receiving which the divine Word does entails his self-emptying. He emptied himself of his divine power in order to receive our human nature. But in order to receive his divinity we do not empty ourselves of our humanity. Some modern commentators have thought that the notion of theosis implies that we do.[4] They see theosis as negating our humanity and accuse the Fathers of getting carried away by the neat symmetry of kenosis-theosis. What we empty ourselves of, however, are the distorted aspects of our fallen human nature so that we can attain to the true fullness of humanity in Christ. As Father Dumitru Stăniloae has put it, "The glory to which man is called is that he should grow more godlike by growing ever more human."[5]

[4]For example, Ben Drewery, "Deification," in Peter Brooks, ed., *Christian Spirituality: Essays in Honour of Gordon Rupp* (London: SCM Press, 1975), 33–62. See also Fergus Kerr's discussion of Martha Nussbaum's "opposition to the aspiration to transcendence that destroys our humanity" and Karl Barth's "fear of any transcendence that destroys our humanity" in Fergus Kerr, *Immortal Longings: Versions of Transcending Humanity* (London: SPCK, 1997), 22; 24. Christian authors have been aware of this fear since antiquity. Cf. St Anastasius of Sinai (died c. 700): "Theosis is the elevation to what is better, but not the reduction of our nature to something less, nor is it an essential change of our human nature . . . [It] is that which has been lifted up to a greater glory, without its own nature being changed" (*Concerning the Word*, PG 89, 77BC, cited by Stavropoulos, *Partakers of the Divine Nature*, 19).

[5]Ware, *Orthodox Way*, 87.

Emptying ourselves of the distorted aspects of our fallen human nature is not a negative work of repression. It is brought about by responding in love to God's gift of himself to us. To quote Father Stăniloae again,

> a gift calls for a responding gift so that the reciprocity of love may be realized. To God, however, man can give back nothing but what has been given him for his needs; his gift, therefore, is sacrifice and he offers it in thanksgiving to God. Man's gift to God is sacrifice and "eucharist" in the widest sense.[6]

It is also "eucharist" in the narrower sense. We cannot achieve theosis on our own. We need the ecclesial community in which we are re-created in the image of God through baptism and the Eucharist. In the Eucharist we give our symbolic gifts to God; he gives us himself in return. Deification is a state of profound communion with God and with each other. Although consummated in the kingdom of heaven, it begins in the worshiping community.

The two Church Fathers who have reflected most deeply on the role of theosis in the economy of salvation are the Alexandrians St Athanasius and St Cyril. The former's saying has already been quoted: "He became human that we might become divine." Athanasius goes on to claim: "he revealed himself through a body that we might receive a conception of the invisible Father; and he endured ignominy from human beings that we might inherit incorruption" (*On the Incarnation*, 54). In other words, to see Christ is to gain insight into divine transcendence. And to enter into his Passion through accepting the Christian way is to gain access to divine life.

[6]Ibid., 85.

Athanasius sees the whole of reality in terms of two opposite polarities: the uncreated Godhead at one pole, and the nothingness from which the world was created at the other. God remains eternally transcendent, but the world is subject to decay and corruption, and it is therefore always being pulled towards the pole of nothingness. Left to our own devices, we would simply unravel and eventually collapse into non-existence. Christ reverses the gravitational pull. In him, and more specifically in the representative humanity which he assumed and deified, transcendence and nearness meet, the uncreated and the created converge. The two poles are drawn together in a state of creative tension. The technical term later given to this is "the communication of idioms." What this means is that divinity is ascribed to the human nature of Christ while humanity is ascribed to his divine nature. The result is a renewal of the human race, a second creation, effected this time from within the human state in the person of Jesus Christ. The *receptivity* of Christ's humanity is vitally important. Unlike our own, his humanity was fully receptive to the Word. Hence within Christ, fallen human nature was reoriented towards the divine.[7]

The representative humanity assumed by Christ at the Incarnation was deified by the Word and exalted through the Passion. This is the cornerstone of Athanasius' narrative of salvation. The next step is how as individual believers we can share in Christ's exalted humanity. The answer is by becoming sons and daughters of God through baptism, so that with the Son of God dwelling within us we can participate in the movement begun by him towards the pole of divine transcendence. That is why for Athanasius the

---

[7]For an excellent discussion, see Khaled Anatolios, *Athanasius: The Coherence of his Thought* (London/New York: Routledge, 1998), passim.

adoption effected by baptism is equivalent to deification. It brings about the renewal of our human nature through participation in the divine nature. It enables us to share in the bond of love uniting the Father and the Son. And finally, in conjunction with the moral life encouraging progress in virtue, it brings us, in the likeness of Christ, to the fullness of the kingdom of heaven.

Athanasius' thinking on the divine economy was completed by Cyril, the great bishop of Alexandria who presided at the Third Ecumenical Council held in Ephesus in 431. The fundamental narrative is the same: the Word created the human race anew in Christ's representative humanity. The divine life of this new humanity is then imparted to us by the Holy Spirit in baptism and through the life-giving body of Christ in the Eucharist. But there are a number of new insights. First, the role of the Holy Spirit is much more fully developed than in Athanasius. It is the Spirit who manifests the eternal plan of God at critical points in the Word's incarnate life. Secondly, Christ in his representative humanity is the recipient as well as the bestower of salvation: "The one who imparts the Spirit as God is the very same one who receives the Spirit as man."[8] Finally, Cyril analyzes with great subtlety our human response to Christ as we grow progressively through the Spirit into the divine image.

The more fully appreciated role of the Holy Spirit is evident in Cyril's exegesis of the gospel accounts of Christ's baptism. Cyril considers the question of why Christ submitted to baptism at all. Did he need it? No. There was nothing in him to be purified. Nor was he an ordinary human being who was to be adopted as the Son of God by the descent of the Spirit. But he accepted—indeed

[8]Daniel A. Keating, *The Appropriation of Divine Life in Cyril of Alexandria* (Oxford: Oxford University Press, 2004), 32.

sought—baptism as a human being representative of all of us. Was his baptism then just to set us an example? No. This would have made Christ's work of salvation simply an external act. Christ was baptized as the *recipient* of salvation, receiving the Spirit on our behalf in virtue of his humanity. This humanity, even though free of sin, still needed to be re-created in the divine image. The image formed in Adam had been lost, not all at once through Adam's "fall," but progressively as the human race gradually became alienated from God (cf. Gen 6.1–8). The baptism of Christ manifests the eternal plan of God accomplished through the Incarnation. In Christ, who is the boundary and link between the human and the divine, the representative recipient of our redemption was transformed by the Holy Spirit.

Christ is also "as man" the example and model for our own sanctification and divinization as individual human beings. This we achieve by participation and grace. As well as receiving sanctification on our behalf (cf. Jn 17.19), Christ also bestows it upon us. By receiving sonship in baptism we become "partakers of the divine nature" (2 Pet 1.4). This text, which was rarely cited before Cyril, is used by him as a kind of shorthand expression for "the new reality the human race possesses in Christ."[9] Cyril does not use Gregory of Nazianzus' term "theosis" to express this new reality. He does not even make much use of Athanasius' term "theopoiesis." For him deification is expressed in a cluster of biblical expressions: justification, sanctification, adoptive sonship, sharing in the Spirit and, above all, partaking of the divine nature. All these are aspects of a single reality: "Properly speaking, *Christ in us*—through his Spirit and life-giving flesh—is the source and

[9]Ibid., 150.

ground of our divinization, accomplishing our justification, our sanctification, our divine filiation, and our participation in the divine nature."[10] Theosis for Cyril is the result of our living with the life of Christ through the power of the Holy Spirit. It is this which accomplishes the working out of the divine economy.

When we turn to the later Fathers we find a somewhat different perspective, one which is more speculative, more focused on the eschatological fulfillment of the Christian in the world to come. The great exponent of this approach is St Maximus the Confessor (c. 580–662). His key idea with respect to the divine economy is that under divine providence the created order is moving from a state of fragmentation to one of unification, and the power which is effecting this unification is love. Through the unifying function of love, says St Maximus, "God and man are drawn together in a single embrace" (*Letter* 2; trans. Louth).

The critical event which has made this unification possible is the Incarnation. Through the Incarnation, Christ manifested God's love, inaugurating a new age in which the corrupting principle introduced into our nature by the Fall was banished. The Incarnation took place "to present nature pure again as from a new beginning, with an additional advantage through deification over the first creation" (*To Thalassius* 54). Christ did not simply restore human nature to its pristine state. He opened up new possibilities for it. By his natural *sarkosis*, or "enfleshing," he brought us a supernatural *theosis*, or "engodding."

Theosis is the working out of the divine economy, the goal of the divine will. In his meditation on the Lord's Prayer, St Maximus

[10]Ibid., 193.

speaks of seven great mysteries which have been introduced by the new dispensation of Christ. These are:

- *theology*, by which we attain knowledge of God through the incarnate Word;

- *adoption as sons and daughters*, which is brought about by baptism and maintained by keeping the commandments;

- *equality with the angels*, which was achieved for us by Christ's sacrifice on the Cross, which united heaven and earth in his person;

- *participation in eternal life*, by feeding on the Word as the bread of life, both through meditating on the Scriptures and through sharing in the Eucharist;

- *restoration of human nature*, by Christ's healing of the interior conflicts of the human will in his representative humanity;

- *abolition of the law of sin*, by which Christ has freed us from the terrible compulsiveness of sin if we freely choose to accept the mystery of salvation; and

- *destruction of the tyranny of the evil one*, which was brought about because the flesh defeated in Adam proved victorious in Christ.

We are almost in a different world here from Athanasius and Cyril. Maximus stands back, as it were, and contemplates the significance of the Incarnation from the perspective of eternity. Commenting to his correspondent, Thalassius, on the meaning of

Ephesians 2.7, "that in the coming ages he might show the immeasurable riches of his grace," he identifies the ages historically as two: one leading up to the Incarnation, the other following it. The first is characterized by the humanization of the divine in the person of Christ, the second by the divinization of the human in the lives of his followers, "the richness of whose glory has not yet been revealed" (*To Thalassius* 22, scholion 2). On the spiritual level, the level of the interior life, the first age is that of the flesh (our active struggle against the passions); the second is that of the spirit (our passive receptivity to divine grace). It is in the second age (in both senses) that we shall experience the transformation of deification by grace, when we shall pass from the limitations of this life to the transcendent glories of the next.

Modern Orthodox approaches

Modern Orthodox theologians have learned from the Fathers to see theosis not as an independent spiritual doctrine—one teaching among many—but as the crowning point of the divine economy. They fall into two groups. One takes its cue from the cosmic theology and philosophical patterning of St Maximus and the later Fathers, the other returns to the more biblical focus of Athanasius and Cyril. As representatives of the first group we may take Sergius Bulgakov, Vladimir Lossky and Andrew Louth, and as representatives of the second Panayiotis Nellas, John Zizioulas and John Behr.

The first approach tends to see deification as the fulfillment in God not simply of humankind but of the entire created order. Bulgakov describes the passage of the world to the fullness of being as occupying three phases:

its *creation* by the Father through the Son in the Holy Spirit; its union with God through the *Incarnation* of the Son sent from the Father, accomplished by the Holy Spirit through the union in Christ of the two natures, divine and human, and, in the latter, of the entire world, which man contains microcosmically; and finally its *transfiguration*, that is, its definitive deification, where the Divine Sophia is made perfectly transparent through the Holy Spirit sent by the Son from the Father.[11]

These three phases do not correspond to successive ages of the Father, the Son and the Holy Spirit (as they do, for example, in the twelfth-century Italian mystic, Joachim of Fiore). Yet in each phase, although the Triadic God is fully in evidence, the leading role passes successively from the Father to the Son and then to the Holy Spirit. Bulgakov presents, like St Maximus, a divine economy leading through the union of the human and the divine in Christ to final deification in the Spirit at the end of time.

We find the same pattern in Vladimir Lossky's *Mystical Theology of the Eastern Church* in the chapters on "Created Being," "The Economy of the Son," and "The Economy of the Holy Spirit." The world was created with man as its articulate point of consciousness, its prophet and high priest, who was intended from the beginning to bring all created being to fulfillment in God. "In his way to union with God, man in no way leaves creatures aside, but gathers together in his love the whole cosmos disordered by sin, that it may at last be transfigured by grace."[12] This gathering

[11]Sergius Bulgakov, *The Bride of the Lamb*, trans. Boris Jakim (Grand Rapids, MI: Eerdmans/Edinburgh: T&T Clark, 2002), 426.

[12]Vladimir Lossky, *The Mystical Theology of the Eastern Church*, (Crestwood, NY: St Vladimir's Seminary Press, 1976), 111.

together constitutes the mystery of the Church: "The entire universe is called to enter within the Church, to become the Church of Christ, that it may be transformed after the consummation of the ages, into the eternal Kingdom of God."[13]

The Son, through the Incarnation, deified the human nature that he assumed. "What must be deified in us is our entire nature, belonging to our person which must enter into union with God, and become a person created in two natures: a human nature which is deified, and a nature or, rather, divine energy that deifies."[14] Christ in his own person created a new type of human nature. This is not the final goal:

> But if in our nature we are members, and parts of the humanity of Christ, our persons have not yet reached union with the Godhead. Redemption and purification of nature do not yet provide all the conditions necessary for deification. The Church is already the Body of Christ, but she is not yet "the fullness of Him who filleth all in all" (Eph 1.23).[15]

The further stage that is needed is the advent of the Holy Spirit. The Holy Spirit has to come to us to make our being the Throne of the Holy Trinity. "Through the coming of the Holy Spirit the Trinity dwells within us and deifies us."[16] But it is the Spirit who has the leading role, for it is he who cries in our hearts, "Abba, Father!" "This is the way of deification leading to the Kingdom of God which is introduced into our hearts by the Holy Spirit,

[13]Ibid., 133.

[14]Ibid., 155.

[15]Ibid., 155.

[16]Ibid., 171.

even in the present life,"[17] Curiously, in the age to come the saints will manifest the image not of the Son but of the Spirit: "It is then that this divine Person, now unknown, not having His image in another hypostasis, will manifest Himself in deified persons: for the multitude of the saints will be His image."[18] The unfolding of the divine economy thus extends into eternity when the Holy Spirit is manifested in the deified people of God as a final phase of revelation.

Andrew Louth follows Bulgakov and Lossky in seeing a cosmic dimension to deification. He also emphasizes its character as an eschatological destiny, "a destiny that finds its fulfillment in a face-to-face encounter with God."[19] For theosis is much more than the remedying of the effects of the Fall. Louth presents this by using the image of an arch, "an arch stretching from creation to deification, representing what is and remains God's intention: the creation of the cosmos that, through humankind, is destined to share in the divine life, to be deified."[20] This Louth calls "the greater arch." He contrasts it with "the lesser arch" from creation to redemption, which he characterizes as the Western perspective. "The greater arch" reveals the full scope of the divine economy, which is to incorporate humankind along with the created world represented by humankind into the life of the Trinity.

The second approach of modern Orthodox scholars is focused more intensely on the incarnate Son. For Panayiotis Nellas, "The

---

[17]Ibid., 173.

[18]Ibid., 173.

[19]Louth, "The Place of *Theosis*," 34.

[20]Ibid., 35.

real anthropological meaning of deification is Christification."[21] Humankind is the image of the Image. Our fulfillment as human beings lies in making this image a living reality by becoming like God—by union with the Logos through the divine energies. Becoming like God implies that we have within us an element of the divine. What exactly is this element? It is what Nellas calls our "theological structure," by which he means our innate capacity for transcending our finitude:

> Having been made in the image of God, man has a theological structure. And to be a true man he must at every moment exist and live theocentrically. When he denies God he denies himself and destroys himself. When he lives theocentrically he realizes himself by reaching out into infinity; he attains his true fulfilment by extending into eternity.[22]

Nellas still breathes the atmosphere of St Maximus. Zizioulas follows Athanasius more closely. For him theosis is equivalent to adoption. He is uncomfortable with an approach which emphasizes the common attributes but does not differentiate sufficiently between the different persons of the Trinity, or rather, which ignores the role of Christ as our sole means of access to the Father:

> *Theosis* is not simply a matter of participating in God's glory and other *natural* qualities, *common to all three persons of the Trinity*; it is also, or rather above all, our recognition and acceptance by the Father as his *sons* by grace, *in and through our incorporation into his only-begotten Son by nature.*[23]

[21]Nellas, *Deification in Christ*, 39.

[22]Ibid., 42.

[23]John Zizioulas, *Communion and Otherness: Further Studies in Person-*

Zizioulas's is a more Christological approach to deification than we find in Lossky, and indeed in all Orthodox writers who give priority to the divine energies. For Zizioulas it is only through the hypostatic union of God and man in Christ that we arrive at theosis. Christ is the model of our true humanity. We become truly human—true persons—only in relation to God through Christ. Deification does not mean that we cease to be human. It means that we acquire our natural identity as human beings only when we come to share in that union of created and uncreated which was raised to the level of personhood in Christ.[24]

For John Behr, too, theosis is equivalent to Christification. It is in contemplating the Passion of Christ that we come face-to-face with God. We are called to be conformed to the image of God. That image is the Christ we encounter in the Scriptures, who, if we will allow him, assimilates us to himself:

> Focused on the person of the crucified and exalted Christ, the image of the invisible God, and guided by the Spirit bestowed by the risen Christ in our interpretation of the scriptures, we are brought into the identity of Christ, becoming his body—incarnating the Word—so that we can also call upon the one God as Abba, Father.[25]

To be in the image of God is not "to be a person in communion, imaging the three persons in communion in heaven."[26] It is to

hood and the Church, ed. Paul McPartlan (London: T&T Clark, 2006), 31, n. 51, emphasis original.

[24]Ibid., 243.

[25]John Behr, The Mystery of Christ: Life in Death (Crestwood, NY: St Vladimir's Seminary Press, 2006), 177.

[26]Ibid., 176.

follow Christ by taking up his Cross in this life and sharing in his glory in the next. This is not to imply that the second Person of the Trinity is to be thought of simply in historical terms. It is a mistake to see the divine economy merely as "salvation history" which begins with the pre-incarnate Word, continues with the incarnate Jesus Christ, and reaches its consummation in the second coming when the saints will be caught up into the life of God. This makes Christ a being in time, like ourselves. What the divine economy does is to manifest the Trinity at a particular point in time from which we can work backwards to make sense of the past and forwards to interpret the future. This particular point in time occurred when the disciples understood the Passion in the light of the Scriptures. It was then that they were able to recognize the exalted Lord in the breaking of bread, to reach out to his coming, and to see the whole of human history in an entirely new manner. Thus Christ does not simply have an existence parallel to ours. With his crucifixion and resurrection he simultaneously creates and redeems a new humanity which is *already* what it will become as it goes to meet its coming Lord.

To conclude. The structural significance of theosis gives it a place in relation to the divine economy which is characteristic of Orthodoxy. Theosis is not simply another word for salvation or sanctification. Whether (following St Cyril) we understand it in terms of our re-creation in the divine image through our acceptance of baptism and participation in the Eucharist, or whether (following St Maximus) we prefer to see it in broader terms as the fulfillment in God of the entire created order, theosis sums up the divine economy. If the Incarnation is the mystery by which the Word makes humanity his own, theosis is the mystery by which, with our cooperation, he makes divinity our own. This is not just a piece of neat theological patterning. When we encounter the crucified and exalted Christ in the Scriptures and in the sacramental life of the Church, he bestows his identity upon us, drawing us into the divine life. In the three chapters that follow, we shall explore in more detail the Scriptural basis for this entry into the likeness of God.

chapter two
THE BIBLICAL
FOUNDATIONS OF THEOSIS

Western writers, particularly those influenced by the great German scholar, Adolf Harnack (1851–1930), have often argued that the Eastern Christian idea of deification was derived from Hellenistic culture and was only later justified by appealing to biblical texts. This is not a view that can be maintained today. Recent studies have shown that the biblical texts used most frequently by the Fathers to support their teaching on deification—Psalm 81.6, "I said you are gods" and 2 Peter 1.4, "partakers of the divine nature"—were consistently interpreted as referring to deification from the beginning.[1]

---

[1]See Carl Mosser, "The Earliest Patristic Interpretations of Psalm 82, Jewish Antecedents, and the Origins of Christian Deification," *Journal of Theological Studies* 56 (2005), 30–74; Stephen Finlan, "Second Peter's Notion of Divine Participation," in Stephen Finlan and Vladimir Kharlamov, eds, *Theosis: Deification in Christian Theology* (Eugene, OR: Pickwick, 2006), 32–50; James Starr, "Does 2 Peter 1:4 Speak of Deification?" in Michael J. Christensen and Jeffrey A. Wittung, ed., *Partakers of the Divine Nature*, 81–92. Cf. also my "'Partakers of the Divine Nature' (2 Peter 1:4) in the Byzantine Tradition."

"I said you are gods"

The quotation from Psalm 81 (Psalm 82 in the Hebrew numbering) is not only the older text but also the more important. "Partakers of the divine nature" (2 Pet 1.4) is very little quoted until taken up by St Cyril of Alexandria in the early fifth century. "I said you are gods," by contrast, is discussed as early as the second century by Justin Martyr, St Irenaeus of Lyons and Clement of Alexandria, who base their interpretation on an already-existing Jewish tradition.

Three verses in particular of Psalm 81 figure prominently in both Jewish and Christian writers:

- "God stands in the assembly of gods; in the midst of them he will judge gods" (verse 1)

- "I said you are gods, and all of you sons of the Most High. But you die like men, and fall as one of the princes" (verses 6 and 7)

The earliest Christian text to refer to these verses is the Gospel of John (late first-century). There the Theologian tells us that Jesus himself quoted verse 6 when accused by the Jews of blasphemy after he had declared: "I and the Father are one." His accusers picked up stones to stone him, and on being challenged to say why, replied:

"We stone you for no good work but for blasphemy; because you, being a man, make yourself God." Jesus answered them, "Is it not written in your law, 'I said, you are gods'? If he called them gods to whom the word of God came (and scripture cannot be broken) do you say of him whom the Father consecrated and sent into the world, 'You are blaspheming,' because I said, 'I am the Son of God'?" (Jn 10.33–36, RSV)

Jesus quotes the psalm, it should be noted, not to prove his divinity (as is often claimed) but to draw attention to the potential sonship of his hearers. When part of a text of scripture is quoted, in this case the first half of verse 6 of Psalm 81, what is implied by the whole text needs to be taken into consideration. The phrase "I said you are gods" is referred by Jesus to "those to whom the word of God came." The full text speaks of the "gods" as the "sons of the Most High" and goes on to say that nevertheless they die like men.

In the early rabbinic tradition these verses were originally addressed either to Adam and Eve at the time of their fall, or to the Israelites in the desert when they had worshiped the golden calf. In both cases the recipients had received the word of God either as the prohibition to eat of the tree of the knowledge of good and evil, or as the ten commandments brought down from Sinai by Moses, and had rejected it. And in both cases the result was death. Adam and Eve were condemned to return to the dust out of which they had been taken (Gen 3.19), and the faithless Israelites in the Sinai desert were put to the sword (Exod. 32.25–29).

Now the word of God had come to the Israelites in the person of Jesus, for "to all who received him, who believed in his name, he gave power to become children of God" (Jn 1.12). In addressing the psalm to his accusers, Jesus, by implication, stands among them as God stands in the assembly of gods (Ps 81.1; cf. Jn 1.26). As gods and sons of the Most High, or as children of God in John's phraseology, they are called to pass from death to life and resurrection (cf. Jn 5.19–28). But those who do not receive him will die in their sins (Jn 8.24)—"you will die like men, and fall as one of the princes," as the psalm puts it (Ps 81.7). Receiving the word of God makes people gods, that is to say, enables them to share in immortality and incorruption. In rejecting it they refuse life and pass into death, falling "as one of the princes." Thus Jesus does more than simply refute his accusers. Certainly, they are wrong in accusing him of blasphemy, but worse than that, by rejecting the Word sent by the Father they are rejecting the opportunity to become "gods"—to attain eternal life.

The Church Fathers not only took over the Jewish Scriptures; they also adopted many of the Jewish interpretations. Psalm 81.6–7 was no exception. The Fathers understood this text to summarize the whole of the divine economy from our creation in Adam to our final consummation in the exalted Christ. In adopting this approach, they were also guided by New Testament writers, especially John and Paul.

One of the leading themes of the Gospel and letters of John is that of Jesus Christ as true life. And this life is divine. For not only does Jesus receive life from the Father but he *is* life itself (Jn 11.25; 14.6). All who participate in him, through baptism and the Eucharist, participate in the divine life. This is analogous to receiving biological life from a human father. Hence believers are called "children of God." The children of God are a new spiritual creation. Just as God breathed the breath of life into Adam's nostrils at the first creation (Gen 2.7), so Christ gave the Spirit to the disciples immediately after the Resurrection at humanity's second creation (Jn 20.22). As children of God we shall be like Christ and see him as he is (1 Jn 3.2). But we also possess the fullness of life here and now.

For the Apostle Paul, the symmetrical relationship between the first and second creations occupies an important place in the pattern of his thought. He sees Christ not only as the agent but also as the recipient of divine action. Hence his presentation of Christ as the second Adam, our solidarity in Adam being mirrored by our solidarity in Christ. Our participation in the new humanity effected in Christ is expressed by the idea of "adoption." Paul is the first to use this term, but he does not pluck it out of the air. The prophet Hosea had already said that once the children of Israel have been restored to faithfulness, they will be called "sons of the living God" (Hos 1.10). Paul builds on this idea. Sonship will only be fully manifested after the resurrection, when what is mortal will be "swallowed up by life" (2 Cor 5.4). But this sonship is also a present reality, because by "adoption" we become fellow-sons and fellow-heirs with Christ, and consequently can address God as "Abba, Father!" (Gal 4.6).

The agent of our adoption is the Spirit, who enables us to share in the suffering of Christ so that we can also share in his glory. Participation in Christ brings about a genuine change in us. Christians really are transformed as they advance from one glory to another (2 Cor 3.18). "In Christ" they put on the new humanity created by Christ. Paul speaks of it using biological images. "I became your father in Christ Jesus through the gospel," he says (1 Cor 4.15). And he goes so far as to describe himself as a woman in labor struggling to bring forth spiritual children "until Christ be formed in you" (Gal 4.19).

We are refashioned through baptism and through being transformed into the image of Christ, which Paul describes as a "new creation" (2 Cor 5.17), what is mortal being "swallowed up by life" so that finally we live with the life of Christ. Paul often speaks of our being "with Christ" and "in Christ." These terms refer to the action of Christ upon us now, when we are incorporated into him through baptism and the acceptance of the Cross, and at the final consummation of things when we shall be associated with him in his resurrected glory.

Those of the early Fathers who take up the rabbinic exegesis of Psalm 81.6–7 integrate it into Paul's theological scheme of dying and rising with Christ. The first is Justin Martyr, who taught in Rome in the mid-second century. Justin refers to the psalm in the course of his *Dialogue with Trypho*. This text is supposed to be an account of a debate with a Jewish scholar called Trypho conducted by Justin at Ephesus in the 140s. The debate is probably a literary fiction, but there is no doubt that Justin, who was born in Nablus in Palestine, was familiar with Jewish teachings. At a certain point, the discussion turns to the identity of the true Israel. Justin argues that the Christians have superseded the Jews: "We are called the true children of God and are such because we keep the commandments of Christ" (*Dialogue with Trypho* 123). He appeals to Psalm 81.6, saying that the words were originally addressed to Adam and Eve, as verse 7 proves. The first human couple were thought worthy of becoming gods (i.e. of sharing in immortality), but they were judged and condemned because of their disobedience. Their defeat, however, has been reversed by the victory of Christ. They failed to become gods and children of God through their disobedience; but Christians have succeeded in becoming precisely that through their obedience to Christ. Conforming to Christ has restored them to Adam's divine state.

Justin implies that this conforming to Christ begins with the new
birth of baptism. But he does not make the connection between
baptism and the gods of Psalm 81 explicit. This was to be done
a few decades later by St Irenaeus of Lyons. In his great work
Against the Heresies, Irenaeus connects the gods of Psalm 81 for
the first time with St Paul's teaching on adoption. Psalm 81.1,
he says ("God stood in the congregation of God, he judges in
the midst of gods"—in the version he used) refers to the Father
and the Son and those who have received the grace of adoption
through which we cry, "Abba, Father!" Where Justin had understood the gods to be those who had been obedient to the Law in
the Jewish fashion (even though it was the Law of Christ), Irenaeus says that Christians had become "gods" through baptism
(*Against the Heresies* 3.6.1).

A little later he moves on to consider verse 7 of the psalm. This,
he says, "was addressed to those who have not received the gift
of adoption." And by failing to honor the Incarnation through
the acceptance of baptism, they have deprived themselves of their
ascent to God (*Against the Heresies* 3.19.1).

When he returns to the psalm a third time, he develops an entirely
new aspect. Here he is looking for an argument against those
who felt that having been baptized they had nothing more to do:
they had attained divinity in one go. No, he said; you have got to
become fully human (i.e. conquer the passions) before you can
become like God. You are not able to receive God's gift of eternal existence without first growing to maturity. When the psalm
says, "you shall die like men" (verse 7), that is to tell us that we
cannot carry the full charge of divinity unless we first grow into
the image and likeness that had been forfeited by Adam. Bap-

tism gives us a potential immortality, but we have to work at it before we can call ourselves "gods and sons of the Most High." Irenaeus thus not only makes the psalm's connection with baptism explicit, but associates it with the recovery of the image and likeness of God (*Against the Heresies* 4.38.3). In other words, to the psalm's connection with the mystery of baptism he adds a moral dimension.

Irenaeus was widely read in antiquity, as we know from an early papyrus fragment of *Against the Heresies* discovered in the sands of Egypt. It was in Egypt (not entirely by coincidence) that the Church's thinking on "gods and sons of the Most High" was carried forward and deepened. Alexandria, on the Egyptian coast near the Nile delta, was the largest city of the Roman Empire after Rome itself and the greatest center of Greek learning. It was to Alexandria that a young Athenian came in about 180 in search of Christian philosophical teaching. This was a younger contemporary of Irenaeus, known to us as Clement of Alexandria (c. 150 to c. 215).

Clement ran a school, or study-circle, in Alexandria and published several books on the Christian life. One of these was the *Paedagogus*, or *Tutor*, intended to help the recently baptized deepen their understanding of the Christian faith. Here Clement follows Irenaeus in connecting Psalm 81.6 with baptism. Christ, he says, at his own baptism in the Jordan was sanctified by the descent of the Holy Spirit:

> The same also takes place in our case, whose exemplar Christ became. Being baptized, we are illuminated; illuminated, we become sons; being made sons, we become perfect; being made perfect we become immortal. "I said," says Scripture,

"you are gods and all of you sons of the Most High." (*Paed.* 1.26.1)

To become "gods and sons of the Most High" means to attain immortal life. In his *Protrepticus*, however, or *Exhortation to the Greeks*, which is addressed to educated Christians and others interested in Christianity, Clement goes further. Here he concludes by saying that the "gods and sons of the Most High" are not simply those whom the Father has adopted through baptism. They are also those who have attained the likeness of God. Irenaeus had already made this connection, but where Clement goes beyond him is to link it with the Platonic axiom (drawn from Plato's dialogue, *Thaeatetus* 176b) that the philosopher's chief task is to become like God as far as possible. Thus only the Christian is the true philosopher, because it is only through baptism in combination with the pursuit of the moral life that likeness to God can be attained.[2]

In the *Stromateis*, a different kind of work which reflects the private teaching in Clement's own school, the baptismal associations of Psalm 81.6 are left behind. The "gods" are those who have risen above the passions. This is in harmony with the best Greek philosophers. Indeed, Clement quotes Empedocles, a philosopher of the fifth century B.C., to confirm that the Christian Gnostic becomes a god even in this life through controlling the soul's lower faculties—not literally but by analogy, for just as we are sons in relation to God as Father, so we are gods in relation to God as Lord.[3]

---

[2]Clement, *Protrepticus* 12. 122.4–12. 125.1

[3]Clement, *Stromateis* 2. 125. 4–5; 4. 149. 8–4. 150.1; 6. 146. 1–2.

The later Fathers are cautious about following Clement down these speculative paths. They are content to accept the reference to baptism along with the moral striving this implies, but as the distinction between Christ and the created order becomes more sharply defined, they are anxious to stress that we do not become gods in a literal sense. Cyril of Alexandria (died 444) speaks for them when he says:

> We therefore ascend to a dignity that transcends our nature
> on account of Christ, but we shall not also be sons of God
> ourselves in exactly the same way as he is, only in relation
> to him through grace by imitation. For he is a true Son who
> has his existence from the Father, while we are his sons who
> have been adopted out of his love for us, and are recipients
> by grace of the text, "I have said, you are gods and all of
> you sons of the Most High" (Ps 81.6). (*Comm. on John*
> 1.9.91bc)

Before we leave this section, it is worth noting that the Fathers did not lose sight of the way Jesus himself had invoked Psalm 81.6. Origen, citing John 10.35, says that the "gods" of Scripture were those "to whom the word came."[4] And for Athanasius (died 373) this aspect provided him with a useful point when arguing for the pre-existence of Christ. If the ancestors of Christ's accusers were "gods" because they were those "to whom the word came," it followed that, since they could only have been gods through him, he pre-existed them all (*Against the Arians* 1.39).

---

[4]e.g. Origen, *Select passages on the Psalms* 135; *Select passages on Ezekiel* 1.3; *Commentary on the Song of Songs*, Prol. 2. 34; *Commentary on Matthew* A 24.

Partakers of the divine nature

The other important biblical text is 2 Peter 1.4, "partakers of the divine nature." This comes from what is perhaps the latest book to be included in the canon of the New Testament. Here is the passage in full:

> By his divine power, he has given us all the things that we need for life and for true devotion, bringing us to know God himself, who has called us by his own glory and goodness. In making these gifts, he has given us the guarantee of something very great and wonderful to come: through them you will be able to share the divine nature and to escape corruption in a world that is sunk in vice. But to attain this, you will have to do your utmost yourselves, adding goodness to the faith that you have, understanding to your goodness, self-control to your understanding, patience to your self-control, true devotion to your patience, kindness towards your fellow men to your devotion, and to this kindness, love.
> (2 Pet 1.3–7)

This translation (from the Jerusalem Bible) makes the relationship between divine action and human response particularly clear. The divine nature (*physis*) in which we are to share through God's gifts is not his essential being but his attributes of glory (*doxa*) and goodness (*aretē*). Such participation brings us from corruption to incorruption (*aphtharsia*), one of the greatest of the divine attributes. But this is not effected automatically. We have to respond to the divine initiative with faith, goodness, understanding, self-control, patience, true devotion, kindness to our fellow human beings, and love. Our admission to the eternal kingdom depends on the moral effort we make. In other words, our sharing in the attributes of divinity is conditional on our fully acquiring the attributes of humanity.

The early Fathers seem wary of this text. The first to quote it is Origen in the mid-third century and it is rarely appealed to again until Cyril finds it useful for his own reasons in the fifth century. Perhaps the Gnostic claim that through self-knowledge we can realize the divine potential within us made 2 Peter 1.4 difficult to handle, although I have not found any evidence that the Gnostics themselves quoted it. Yet the Fathers were aware of the powerful attraction of Gnosticism. The spiritual teaching of Origen was intended in part to make orthodox Christianity just as attractive to educated Christians. In his treatise *On First Principles* he advises us to follow the example of Christ, so that "by this means we may as far as is possible become, through our imitation of him, partakers of the divine nature" (*On First Principles* 4.4.4). In this context the divine nature is defined as intellectual light. Elsewhere it is wisdom, righteousness, goodness, immortality and incorruption. Imitating Christ, through following him along "the steep path of virtue," enables us to replicate the divine attributes within ourselves. Not that we are able to achieve this by our own effort. Participation is simultaneously a divine gift. The Holy Spirit makes us holy and spiritual so that the divine Son can make us sons and gods. The Son, like leaven, transforms us into himself. Yet we do not become the same thing as the Son is, for partaking of the divine nature implies a relationship between that which exists in its own right (He who Is) and that which exists only in a contingent or dependent sense (ourselves). If one reality participates in another, the one that is doing the participating cannot be equal to the one in which it participates.

We next find 2 Peter 1.4 in the writings of Athanasius the Great. Taking his cue from Origen, St Athanasius uses the verse to support the idea of the believer's dynamic participation in a personal God, but with a different emphasis. It is not our imitation of Christ through the pursuit of virtue that is important now but our access to the Father through the Son, made possible by the Incarnation and appropriated by us through baptism.

This is built on, in turn, by St Cyril of Alexandria, who completes the patristic interpretation of 2 Peter 1.4 by deepening our understanding of how our human nature is exalted and transformed in Christ:

> How are we "God's offspring" (Acts 17.29)? [says Cyril] In what way are we "partakers of the divine nature" (2 Pet 1.4)? We do not limit our boast merely to the fact that Christ wished to take us into an intimate relationship with him. No, the truth of the matter is evident to us all. For "the divine nature" is God the Word together with the flesh. And we are his "offspring" even though he is God by nature, on account of his taking the same flesh as ourselves. Therefore the mode of the relationship rests on likeness. For just as he is intimately related to the Father, and the Father through the identity of the nature is intimately related to him, so we too are intimately related to him—in that he became man—and he to us. We are united to the Father through him as through a mediator. For Christ is, so to speak, a frontier between supreme divinity and humanity, since both are present within him. And containing within him, as it were, two such very different things, he is united on the one hand to God the Father, since he is God by nature, and on the other

to human beings, since he is truly human. (*Comm. on John* 6.1, 653de)

Christ raises us to intimacy with the Father because he shares his being with the Father in one sense and with us in another. Baptism into Christ through the Spirit enables us to participate in the very life of the triadic God.

In Cyril's later writings "partaking of the divine nature" replaces "deification" (*theopoiēsis*) as a convenient way of referring to the goal of human life. Why this is so is not entirely clear, but it seems prompted by pressure from more than one quarter. In his Festal Letter of 425 he answers Jewish accusations that Christians worshiped a deified human being. And in 429 he attacks Nestorius, at that time still archbishop of Constantinople, for complaining that Christians who speak of the deification of the flesh assumed by Christ at the Incarnation are advocating a kind of apotheosis.[5] From the mid-420s he prefers to use the phrase "partakers of the divine nature" which neatly balances his emphasis on Christ's partaking of our human nature.

After Cyril we do not find much reference in the Fathers to 2 Peter 1.4. In the Byzantine Church the emphasis falls on the apophatic

[5] In *Against Nestorius* II.8. The passage is given in translation in my *Cyril of Alexandria* (London and New York: Routledge, 2000), 152. The Alexandrians by this time had long been accustomed to speaking of the flesh assumed by the Word at the Incarnation as deified by him. For a theologian of an Antiochene background, such as Nestorius, this sounded strange. It seemed to imply that the human nature of Christ was absorbed into the divine nature—hence Nestorius's "apotheosis." In fact, even perfectly orthodox Fathers originating from Antioch, such as St John Chrysostom, did not like to use deification language. (See further, my *Doctrine of Deification*, 237.)

nature of God—the radical inaccessibility of his essential being—
as advocated by Dionysius the Areopagite and Maximus the
Confessor. It is only with St Gregory Palamas that "partakers
of the divine nature" once again becomes important in theological debate. Palamas's opponents argued that it proved that the
saints could share in the divine essence, thus making any talk of
divine energies redundant. Palamas responded by agreeing that
the saints receive the whole of God but maintaining that he still
remained inaccessible in his essence because what they shared in
was his divine energies.

Other biblical approaches

The Fathers' teaching on theosis arose initially out of their exegesis of Psalm 81.6. It was later confirmed by 2 Peter 1.4, although
only St Cyril of Alexandria made extensive use of the Petrine
text. This teaching was not, however, based narrowly on Psalm
81 and 2 Peter. It developed as the Fathers sought to unfold the
meaning of the divine economy largely against the background
of the Apostle Paul's thought. Once theosis had been established
in this way as the goal of human life, it could be found throughout Scripture by employing typological and symbolic methods of
interpretation.

Modern Orthodox writers have tended to see theosis as implied
not so much by specific texts as by the overall structure of the
Bible. An interesting recent book by a British scholar, Stephen
Thomas, looks first at the Old Testament as an assurance to us
that in spite of our damaged humanity Paradise can be regained,
and then shows how in the New Testament this damaged humanity is restored to divine glory in and through Christ. By immers-

ing ourselves in the biblical narrative, and discerning there the main lines of the divine economy—what Thomas calls "the big picture"—we can begin to appropriate the divine life. This is not a matter of acquiring information from the Bible; it is actively engaging with the God who is revealed in it. "To read the Bible, then, is not only to gain guidance about how to be deified: it is actually *part of the process* of our deification, as we are led up into the presence of God through human signs."[6]

What Thomas is attempting to do is to reintroduce us to a patristic way of reading the Bible, using (in an updated fashion) the traditional three senses of Scripture: the historical, the moral and the spiritual. With some of the Fathers the spiritual sense relies largely on allegory. This can be most illuminating. St Maximus, for example, finds in the story of the Wedding Feast at Cana (Jn 2.6) a wealth of suggestive details. The six stone jars illustrate the divine economy. They were empty because humanity had squandered God's gifts in pursuit of material goals. When they were refilled, the water was changed into wine, which symbolizes our receiving a knowledge that transcends nature. The good wine that came last is the eschatological transformation of nature by God's deifying power, bringing a supernatural joy (*To Thalassius* 40). Thomas accepts such allegorical readings as helpful so long as the spiritual sense expresses our relationship to the Father in the Son through the Holy Spirit:

> The spiritual sense of the Bible . . . makes clear that Christology should never be separated from Trinitarian theology. If we read *Christologically*, with Christ as the key, and *pneu-*

---

[6]Stephen Thomas, *Deification in the Eastern Orthodox Tradition: A Biblical Perspective* (Piscataway, NJ: Gorgias Press, 2007), 74.

matically, with the Holy Spirit's energies in our hearts and minds, the Bible acts upon us "anagogically": *it leads us up to God the Father.*[7]

Reading the Bible with the eyes of faith in itself opens us up to the deifying power of the Holy Spirit's divine energies, because Christ is present throughout the sacred text.

Father John Behr also wants us to reengage with the Scriptures. But his emphasis is rather different. As we saw in the previous chapter, he focuses on the Cross, looking backwards from that point to creation and forwards to the consummation of all things in the glorified Christ. Reflection on Christ according to the Scriptures begins with the crucifixion. By "searching the Scriptures" like the apostles, we recognize the crucified and exalted one as an eschatological figure who is advancing to meet us. We are able to be "born again to be the body of Christ."[8] This rebirth is an ongoing process for us, for what we shall be is still not revealed. But we know we shall be like Christ, and because "*what* we see in Christ, as proclaimed by the apostles, is *what* it is to be God"[9] we shall ourselves be gods by grace.

[7]Ibid., 86, emphasis original.

[8]Behr, *The Mystery of Christ*, 18.

[9]Ibid., 174.

chapter three

IMAGE AND LIKENESS

The story of creation that opens the book of Genesis reaches its climax with the creation of human life:

> Then God said, "Let us make humankind in our image, according to our likeness; and let them have dominion over the fish of the sea, and over the birds of the air, and over the cattle, and over all the wild animals of the earth, and over every creeping thing that creeps upon the earth." So God created humankind in his image, in the image of God he created them; male and female he created them. (Gen 1.26–28, New RSV)

In these verses we are presented with a theological anthropology which is as valid today as when it was first revealed. Humankind is defined in relation to God. We are not autonomous beings that can discover the meaning of life simply by reference to ourselves. "For the human soul," says St Tikhon of Zadonsk (1724–1783), "is a spirit made by God, and only in God, by whom it was made in his image and likeness, can it discover contentment, repose, peace, solace and joy."[1]

---

[1]Cited in Vladimir Lossky, *Orthodox Theology: An Introduction* (Crestwood, NY: St Vladimir's Seminary Press, 1978), 131.

What, then, is this divine image and likeness that we were created to reflect? The book of Genesis seems to suggest that it is chiefly dominion over the rest of creation, that is to say, that we image God because we share in his sovereignty and power. Later writers, both Jewish and Christian, enlarge this idea to include a number of other divine attributes. "God created man for incorruption," says the Book of Wisdom, "and made him in the image of his own eternity" (Wis 2.23). For Cyril of Alexandria the image is manifested in our capacity for goodness, righteousness and holiness (*Dogmatic Solutions* 3). For John Climacus it lies in our ability to resemble God in his divine love (*Spiritual Ladder*, Step 30). The image is thus a God-given potentiality for sharing in the divine life. Or, as Lossky puts it, the image is the principle of God's self-manifestation, the foundation of a particular relationship with him.[2]

The anthropomorphite controversy

The Church did not arrive at this understanding without a long struggle. At the turn of the fifth century a controversy arose about the nature of the divine image. It began in 399 when Archbishop Theophilus Alexandria, in his Festal Letter for Easter of that year, criticized (innocently enough) "certain people of the more rustic and uncultivated sort" for holding that "it was necessary to conceive of God in human form" (*Letter from Constantinople*, frag. 7). He argued that the image of God in humankind was not corporeal, but reflected the divine attributes of immortality and incorruptibility and had therefore been lost with the Fall.

[2]Vladimir Lossky, *In the Image and Likeness of God* (Crestwood, NY: St Vladimir's Seminary Press, 1974), 126.

This letter caused dismay among many of the Egyptian monks. Few of them had had the kind of education that would have enabled them to locate the divine image in abstract principles rather than in the human form which God created out of the dust from the ground and animated by breathing into it the breath of life (cf. Gen 2.7). To say that the image was lost by the Fall seemed to them to open up an unbridgeable chasm between humankind and God. St John Cassian, who was living in Egypt at the time, at the monastic settlement of Scetis, describes how a monk called Sarapion broke down and wept, crying: "They have taken my God from me" (*Conferences* 10.2). Other monks were more militant and mounted a violent demonstration in Alexandria against their archbishop. To pacify them Theophilus had to back down and concede that Adam had not forfeited the divine image through the Fall.[3]

Most of the monks were steeped in the Bible and the apocalyptic literature popular at the time that described the heavenly world in very graphic physical terms. They were suspicious of the small group of intellectuals who followed the spiritual teaching of the controversial third-century Father, Origen of Alexandria, and felt that by denying that the human form was in the image of God Theophilus was taking their side. Origen's teachings had been refined in the course of the fourth century by other Fathers, notably the great theorist of the monastic life, Evagrius of Pontus (died 399). Evagrius was against thinking about God in any human terms at all. One of the features of his teaching was that if prayer is to be effective, not only the passions but any picturing in the imagination, even picturing of the divine, must be suppressed, for

[3]For a more detailed account see my *Theophilus of Alexandria* (London and New York: Routledge, 2007), 18–27.

mental images only lead to delusion and even insanity. This was an austere teaching indeed:

> When you pray, do not form images of the divine within yourself, nor allow your mind to be impressed with any form, but approach the Immaterial immaterially and you will come to understanding.

> Blessed is the mind which becomes immaterial and free from all things during the time of prayer. (*Chapters on Prayer* 66 and 119; trans. Sinkewicz)

In the highest experience of prayer, which transcends all words and images, the mind is flooded with divine light. Byzantine monasticism, as we shall see, was able to integrate Evagrius's teaching on imageless prayer with a conviction that we have been created in the image and likeness of God. But in the early fifth century it seemed to many that the two ideas were mutually exclusive. Theophilus tried to steer a middle course, condemning the "Origenists" on the one hand as too speculative, and the "Anthropomorphites" on the other for making God too much like a created human being. But the controversy was not to be settled that easily. It was not until the middle of the sixth century that an ecumenical council, faced with the resurgence of an esoteric form of Origenism—which held, among other things, that the spiritual elite become equal to Christ ("Isochrists")—finally condemned both Origen and Evagrius. Fortunately for the monastic tradition, Evagrius' writings continued to be read, often through the simple expedient of reassigning authorship to an approved Father, and they are still influential today. What, then, should we make of the divine image?

The Fathers on the image and likeness

In his Festal Letter of 399 Theophilus was simply following the teaching of his great predecessor, Athanasius. Athanasius does not make a distinction between "image" and "likeness"; he distinguishes only between "Image" and "in the image." For the Son alone is the image of the Father. We were created "in the image" because our ultimate fulfillment lies in our participating in the Son's relation to the Father. We are therefore merely "images of the Image" in Athanasius' view. This respects the teaching of Genesis but at the same time maintains an immense gulf between our created nature and the nature of the uncreated godhead. Only through the incarnate Christ can we approach the Father, who is beyond all human imagining.

What none of the parties in the Anthropomorphite controversy realized was that there was more than one tradition on the image and likeness. Unlike Athanasius, in fact, the majority of the Fathers make a distinction between the image and the likeness, seeing the image as referring to the rational nature we were born with, while the likeness refers to the moral quality we acquire in the course of our Christian life.

This approach goes back to Philo of Alexandria, a Jewish older contemporary of St Paul, who held in the Platonic fashion that the body was simply a dwelling-place for the rational soul, which is "a holy image, of all images the most godlike" (*On Flight and Invention* 69). All the Fathers who make a distinction between image and likeness tend, like Philo, to locate the image in the higher, or rational, part of the human soul. Clement of Alexandria, for example, says that we were created in the image of God but do not receive the likeness, which was lost at the Fall, until we attain perfection (*Stromateis* 2.131.5). Basil the Great says that we already have the image by the fact of being human. Our task as Christians is to acquire the likeness by living a moral life.[4] St John Damascene, writing in the early eighth century, sums up this whole approach. He says that the image lies in our mind and will. The Fall destroyed the likeness in us. But because we retained the image, we still have the basis for regaining it. St John integrates this regaining of the likeness with the economy of salvation. Christ "took on himself a share in our poor and weak nature to cleanse us and make us incorruptible, and establish us once more as partakers of his divinity" (*On the Orthodox Faith* 4.13). So although the likeness is recovered by acquiring virtue "so far as is possible," this is only possible within the context of a sacramental life that incorporates us into Christ. By partaking of the mysteries, we partake of the divinity of Christ in anticipation of our future state, when we shall be able to contemplate him in perfect likeness to him.

By contrast, Basil's brother, St Gregory of Nyssa, does not distinguish between the image and the likeness. We were created on the model of God's sovereign goodness, but we lost that goodness through sin. We are like people who have slipped in the mud and made ourselves unrecognizable by becoming caked in filth. What we need to do to recover our original state is to reverse the process, washing away the image we have made for ourselves by leading a pure life: "When the earthly veil is stripped off, the beauty of the soul stands revealed once more."[5] Such a recovery of beauty

---

[4]Basil the Great, *On the Creation of Man*, PG 44.273D—attributed to Gregory of Nyssa but generally recognized to be Basil's.

[5]Gregory of Nyssa, *On Virginity*, PG 46. 368–376 (the whole passage is translated in Nellas, *Deification in Christ*, 207–210).

marks a return to what is really our natural state as human beings. It is to enter once more into intimacy with God, to participate in his goodness and beauty. And since this goodness and beauty is infinite, our progress in it is eternal: it "has no stopping place but stretches out with the limitless."[6]

Neither do the great Alexandrian bishops, Athanasius, Theophilus and Cyril, distinguish between the image and the likeness. But whereas Gregory's teaching reflects a Christian adaptation of Platonism, the Alexandrians set their discussion firmly in the context of Christ and the Church. Athanasius and Theophilus held that we were created in the image of Christ, who is himself the Image of the Father. Cyril denies that we merely become images of the Image. He teaches that because the Father, Son, and Holy Spirit are so intimately interrelated, when we have the Spirit and the Son, we also have the Father. Cyril is therefore more Trinitarian that his episcopal predecessors in his thinking about the divine image. He is also more willing to see the human personality as an integral whole. For him, the divine image is not to be identified with our rational faculty; it is located in our will. And because our will became distorted through the Fall, we lost the divine image and likeness—one and the same thing for Cyril—at the same time. The Christian life is therefore a progressive sanctification in Christ through the Holy Spirit until we arrive at a full recovery of the divine image. We are thus recreated in Christ by the Holy Spirit so that we can share in the divine attributes of holiness, righteousness and freedom from corruption and decay, attributes which originate in the Father. Recovering the image is equivalent to being deified, not by some external imitation of Christ, or by a divinizing contemplation of

[6]Gregory of Nyssa, *Life of Moses* 7 (trans. A. J. Malherbe and E. Ferguson, Classics of Western Spirituality, 31).

the godhead, but by participating fully in the sacramental life of the ecclesial community. Cyril's vision of the recovery of the divine image in all its dimensions was all but forgotten after his death but has become important again in modern times.

The monastic tradition

The ascetic (or "neptic") Fathers who have reflected on the image and likeness are for the most part those who in the eighteenth century were collected in the *Philokalia*. The monastic tradition they represent is remarkable for its unity of outlook. Although their writings span nearly a thousand years, on the subject of the image and likeness they all support one another. Their teaching can be stated simply:

- the image resides in the soul, or in its highest part, the intellect; it is part of humanity's created structure

- the likeness is a moral quality; it is attained as a result of ascetic effort

This is not to say that the body is ignored. It is only through its union with the body that the soul is capable of attaining the divine likeness at all. St Maximus, for example, teaches that the soul's "intelligent provision for the lower part" makes the body its "fellow servant."[7] Body and soul together are constitutive of the human person, which finds its perfection (in the sense of completion) in the divine likeness.

---

[7]*Ambiguum* 7, PG 91. 1092B; Adam G. Cooper, *The Body in St Maximus the Confessor: Holy Flesh, Wholly Deified* (Oxford: Oxford University Press, 2005), 109. Cooper's whole discussion of corporeality in St Maximus is very helpful.

The monk's passage from image to likeness is so central to the ascetic tradition that Abba Philemon (late 6th/early 7th cent.) can describe the hesychast as one who "guards the divine image in himself and enriches his likeness to God."[8] So much of the teaching of the *Philokalia* is directed towards this end. And not only of the *Philokalia*: St John Climacus insists in *The Ladder of Divine Ascent* that we are all—not just the monks—bound to strive to attain the divine image: "Indeed everyone should struggle to raise his clay, so to speak, to a place on the throne of God" (*Ladder*, Step 26). Theosis is not an optional extra just for the professionals.

The nature of the contrast between the image and the likeness is vividly described by Diadochus of Photice (5th cent.). It resembles the difference, he says, between the preliminary sketch for a portrait and the finished painting. The image is simply an outline. When the colors are applied, the likeness is brought out and the sitter comes to life, even down to the way he or she smiles.[9] Not that any of the neptic Fathers suggest that the work of attaining the likeness is as easy as having one's portrait painted. "By way of trials and sufferings we must purify the divine image in us," says Abba Philemon, if we are "to receive understanding and the likeness of God."[10] According to St Neilos the Ascetic (5th cent.), it is by battling against the passions that the monk "tries to build a temple of God out of souls made in the divine image."[11] An elev-

[8]Abba Philemon, *Philokalia* ii. 354.

[9]Diadochus of Photice, *Spiritual Knowledge* 78 and 89, *Philokalia* i. 280, 288.

[10]Abba Philemon, *Philokalia* ii. 350.

[11]Neilos the Ascetic, *Ascetic Discourse*, *Philokalia* i. 227.

enth-century writer, Niketas Stethatos, teaches that "we are in His likeness if we possess virtue and understanding."[12] The likeness is not to be attained without the struggle for holiness.

Yet the likeness is also the work of grace. Diadochus assures us that although our cooperation is required, "the perfecting of this likeness we shall know only by the light of grace."[13] It implies our being mingled with God through the Holy Spirit. As a result of this, the intellect enters into an extraordinary intimacy with God, preserving its likeness to him by dwelling among divine realities. We are told indeed by Peter of Damascus (12th cent.), in a manner strongly reminiscent of Evagrius, that "when the intellect is taken up into God it becomes formless and imageless."[14] According to the neptic Fathers, because of its dazzling beauty the likeness bestowed by God leaves the image far behind.

It is not surprising that for the Fathers of the *Philokalia* the divine likeness is only for the few. "All men are made in God's image," says Diadochus, "but to be in His likeness is granted only to those who through great love have brought their own freedom into subjection to God."[15] For Maximus the Confessor, "only the good and the wise attain His likeness."[16] And for John Damascene "only a few—those who are virtuous and holy, and have imitated the goodness of God to the limit of human powers—posses that

[12]Niketas Stethatos, *On Spiritual Knowledge* 11, *Philokalia* iv. 142.

[13]Diadochus of Photice, *Spiritual Knowledge* 89, *Philokalia* i. 228.

[14]Ilias the Presbyter 44, *Philokalia* iii. 49; Peter of Damascus, *Philokalia* iii. 135.

[15]Diadochus of Photice, *Philokalia* i. 253.

[16]Maximus the Confessor, *Chapters on Love* 3. 25, *Philokalia* ii. 87.

which is according to the likeness of God."[17] This is not meant
to be discouraging. Everybody has the opportunity to attain the
divine likeness, but as the Lord himself said, "the gate is narrow
and the road is hard that leads to life, and there are few who find
it" (Mt 7.14).

Some of those few are still to be encountered today in Orthodox
monasticism. St Silouan of Mount Athos was one such. Another
was an anonymous monk described by Archimandrite Vasileios
in his collection of monastic essays, *Hymn of Entry*:

> The light that shines from the genuine monk is a light that
> reveals. It resembles the presence of Christ . . . Such monks,
> unknown and anonymous, but full of light, exist. I know
> one . . .
>
> He has a treasure of inexpressible joy hidden in an earthen
> vessel, small and fragile. And this joy overflows and spreads
> all around him, filling his surroundings with its fragrance.
> Light shines from his being. His inner rejoicing sometimes
> goes beyond his endurance, breaks his heart, shows itself in
> tears and cries and gestures . . .
>
> The uncreated Spirit who has made His dwelling in his heart
> gives meaning and substance to the things within him and
> around him—the uncreated Spirit who is much more tan-
> gible, more truly existing than the landscape around us. And
> the man's body is rendered transparent, full of light.
>
> He is nature and holiness, perfect man and perfect god by
> grace. He does nothing which is false. He does not make

[17]John Damascene, *On the Virtues and Vices, Philokalia* ii. 341.

things, he causes things to be begotten and to proceed. He
does not speak, he acts. He does not comment, he simply
loves.[18]

This remarkable passage echoes many points made by hesychast
authors, particularly by St Gregory Palamas, who speaks of a "fervent and ardent love" that "draws to itself the mystical and ineffable glory of God's nature."[19] The soul is deiform in its capacity
to become threefold while remaining single (that is to say, when
its noetic, rational and sensory powers are all in perfect harmony
with each other) and is thus able on the one hand to ascend to
union with the Triadic Unity, and on the other to draw down the
divine glory to itself.[20] It is the soul's triune nature which enables
Archimandrite Vasileios to assimilate the deified monk to the
Father himself in such a way that the monk causes things "to be
begotten and to proceed." It is then, as St Gregory says, that "the
soul truly possesses the image and likeness of God and is thereby
made gracious, wise and divine."[21]

Such mystical heights are beyond the reach of most monks. What
is more normal in monastic writing is to distinguish between the
experience of God here and now and the divine likeness still to
come. Thus in his account of the teaching of St Silouan of Mount
Athos (1866–1938), Archimandrite Sophrony says:

[18]Archimandrite Vasileios, *Hymn of Entry: Liturgy and Life in the Orthodox
Church* (Crestwood, NY: St Vladimir's Seminary Press, 1984), 126–129.

[19]Gregory Palamas, *150 Chapters* 40, *Philokalia* iv. 364.

[20]Gregory Palamas, *Three Texts on Prayer and Purity of Heart* 2, *Philokalia*
iv. 341.

[21]Gregory Palamas, *150 Chapters* 40, *Philokalia* iv. 364.

To man has been given the hope of receiving in the world to come the gift of Divine likeness and full beatitude. The best he can have in this world, however, is a pledge of this future state. Within the confines of his earthly experience it is given to him to be able during prayer to dwell in God while remembering the world. But when he arrives at a more complete abiding in God the "world is forgotten," just as a man who "cleaves to the earth" with his whole self forgets God.[22]

The wisdom of the neptic Fathers and more recent saints continues to inspire men and women ascetics to build on the divine image through prayer, love and humility until they realize the divine likeness in themselves "so far as is humanly possible," anticipating in this life the beatitude of the world to come.

But what of the rest of us? Is the attainment of the likeness only for monastics who have subjected the body to a rigorous ascetical program, who have systematically subordinated it to spiritual priorities? There are those who think that a negative approach to the body is built into Orthodoxy. "Spiritualization," Hans Urs von Balthasar has said, "is the basic tendency of the patristic epoch."[23] Against this view we should set the tradition represented by Climacus' comment that we should all struggle to raise our clay to a place on the throne of God (*Ladder*, Step 26). It has recently been pointed out that the tension is not "between the spiritual and material per se" but between "an eschatologically oriented order

---

[22]Archimandrite Sophrony, *St Silouan the Athonite*. Crestwood, NY: St Vladimir's Seminary Press, 1999), 114.

[23]Hans Urs Von Balthasar, "The Fathers, the Scholastics and Ourselves," *Communio* 24 (1997), 375; cited by Cooper, *The Body in St Maximus the Confessor*, 5.

(taxis)" and "the chaotic element in material diversity"—that is to say, between matter subjected to the divine ordering introduced by the Incarnation and matter governed by the chaos that has prevailed since the Fall.[24] The tension is resolved not by ignoring or marginalizing the body but by incorporating it into Christ. "Deified creation already exists 'wholly deified' as the body of Christ."[25] All believers can share in this deified creation corporeally through sharing in the body of Christ.

A monastic writer who brings the body very fully into the "eschatologically oriented order" is St Symeon the New Theologian. In his famous "Hymn 15" he describes how our bodies become wholly penetrated by Christ in every detail. He looks at his hand or his foot and sees the hand or foot of Christ: "I move my hand, and it is the whole Christ who is my hand. . . . I move my foot, and behold, it shines like He does himself."[26] In effect, "he who is ashamed of his body is ashamed of God himself."[27] This spiritual transformation (not dematerialization) of the body takes place through the Eucharist. St Symeon received Communion daily throughout his monastic life. For those who had arrived at a state of repentance he advocated daily attendance at the Liturgy and reception of Christ's body and blood: "Blessed are those who are nourished with Christ every day."[28] The monastic life may

[24]Cooper, *The Body in St Maximus the Confessor*, 5–6.

[25]Ibid., 251.

[26]Symeon the New Theologian, *Hymn* 15. 105–106; cited by Alfeyev, *St Symeon the New Theologian and Orthodox Tradition* (Oxford: Oxford University Press, 2000), 266 (trans. modified).

[27]Ibid., 267.

[28]Symeon the New Theologian, *Ethical Discourses* 10.790–91; cited in ibid., 87.

have provided an environment particularly conducive to the daily reception of the Eucharist, but St Symeon also attracted a large following of laypeople.

Modern theologians

The monastic writers have a practical purpose in what they teach. Other theologians are more concerned to place the image within the broader structures of Christian thought. Few have given the topic more consideration than Vladimir Lossky. In his view, if we ignore the teaching of the Fathers on the divine image, we distort the fundamental meaning of Christianity itself:

> There is no branch of theological teaching which can be entirely isolated from the problem of the image without danger of severing it from the living stock of Christian tradition. We may say that for a theologian of the catholic tradition in the East and in the West, for one who is true to the main lines of patristic thought, the theme of the image (in its twofold acceptation—the image as the principle of God's self-manifestation and the image as the foundation of a particular relationship of man to God) must belong to the "essence of Christianity."[29]

The two aspects of the image that Lossky identifies as summarizing the essence of Christianity are:

- a movement from God to ourselves through his self-revelation in Christ;

- a movement from ourselves to God through our response in freedom and love.

[29]Lossky, *In the Image and Likeness of God*, 126.

The image is therefore not a "thing" that we can point to. It is a relationship and, moreover, a relationship that constitutes us as true persons. Metropolitan John Zizioulas underlines this when he says that the image of God is to do with the *how*, not the *what*, of what man is.[30] We exist as personal beings confronting a personal God, mirroring God, as Christos Yannaras puts it, in our personal uniqueness and dissimilarity: "Personal distinctiveness *forms the image* of God in man. It is the *mode of existence* shared by God and man, the *ethos* of trinitarian life imprinted upon the human being."[31] It is important that the body is not excluded, for we know ourselves only as embodied beings. Following many of the Fathers, Yannaras sees the depreciation of the body as harmful to our spiritual wholeness. The soul and the body are not in opposition to each other but are simply two different modes of our *personal* existence.

At this point we have to be careful not to fall into the old error of anthropomorphism, imagining God simply as a bigger and better version of ourselves—of our own ego, that is to say, not of our physical form. God is not made in our image, but we in his. Lossky says, paradoxically, that the image of God in man is unknowable. And Dumitru Stăniloae emphasizes that human beings, in virtue of being made in the divine image, reflect even the apophatic—the unknowable—aspect of God. In their inner depths human beings are as mysterious as God.

Part of this mystery is that although finite beings, we can have a relationship of the most tender intimacy with the utterly infinite and transcendent. What links us to God is our creation in his

---

[30]Zizioulas, *Communion and Otherness,* 165.

[31]Yannaras, cf. his *Freedom of Morality,* 23, *Person and Eros,* §17.

---

image. "Having been created in the image of the infinite God," says Panayiotis Nellas, means that man "is called by his own nature—and this is precisely the sense of 'in the image' from this point of view—to transcend the limited boundaries of creation and to become infinite."[32] "Becoming infinite" might seem to be going beyond what is permissible for us. But this statement only takes up St Gregory of Nyssa's point that because God is infinite, our progress in him is inexhaustible. "God is the source of power and light who draws us always higher up into knowledge and perfection of life," says Stăniloae. "He is not a ceiling that puts an end to our ascent."[33]

The image of God protects both "the mystery of the mode of divine existence" and simultaneously "its imprint in human existence."[34] This imprint is of a triadic character. We bear in our nature traces of the communion that exists between the persons of the Trinity. It has been questioned whether the personal character and self-transcending openness of the image, as taught by the theologians we are considering, can really be found in the Fathers. Is it not something borrowed from more modern philosophical trends? It is true that the personalist philosophy touched on in Chapter II has supplied our theologians with some of their vocabulary. But the substance of their teaching is rooted in the Fathers. One Father particularly close to their perspective is St Cyril of Alexandria. Our acknowledgement that God is triadic, says St Cyril, that "the fullness of the ineffable Godhead is to be understood as present

---

[32]Nellas, *Deification in Christ,* 28.

[33]Dumitru Stăniloae, *The Experience of God,* trans. Ioan Ionita and Robert Barringer vol. i, *Revelation and Knowledge of the Triune God* (Brookline, MA: Holy Cross Orthodox Press, 1994), 107.

[34]Yannaras, *Person and Eros,* 49.

in the holy and consubstantial Trinity," means that our being in the image is also triadic, "that we are conformed to the true and exact image of the Father, that is, to the Son, and that his divine beauty is impressed on our souls through participation in the Holy Spirit."[35] The radiance of this beauty was dimmed by the Fall. But we can gradually recover it by reaching up through the Spirit, in Christ, to the Father, until we come to share fully in the holiness of the Trinity.

Cyril, as we have seen, does not differentiate between the image and the likeness. Our modern theologians, guided principally by St Maximus and St Gregory Palamas, have found it helpful to do so. Stăniloae speaks for them all when he says:

> The Fathers saw in holiness a great likeness of man with God through purification from the passions and through the virtues which culminate in love. But inasmuch as both the cleansing from passions and the virtues can only be acquired through the energy of the grace which strengthens human powers, likeness also means a radiation of the presence of God from within man. In those who love one another and are found within a reciprocal interiority, the face of the one is stamped with the features of the other and these features shine forth actively from within him. Now inasmuch as these divine features are growing and foreshadow the full degree in which they will overwhelm the human features, the faces of the saints even here on earth have something of the eschatological plane of eternity in their appearance, that plane through which God's features will be fully reflected and his energies will radiate.[36]

[35]Cyril of Alexandria, *Against Julian* 1. 33.

[36]Stăniloae, *The Experience of God*, vol. i, 226.

The likeness is the fulfillment of the image, the human being's communion with the persons of the Trinity in freedom and love. In the saints this communion is expressed in the way God's glory is reflected in their faces, in anticipation of the age to come when they will "transcend the limited boundaries of creation" and subsist "in precisely the manner in which God also subsists as being."[37]

The teaching of the Fathers on the image and likeness is central to Orthodox thinking on theosis. The image sets out what we might call the ontological (or "structural") basis of our relationship with God, for no personal relationship can exist when absolutely nothing is shared in common. In the words of Christos Yannaras, "When . . . Scripture says that God blew his own breath in the earthly face of man, this image is to demonstrate the communication to man of certain marks of the very existence of God."[38] The *image* gives us the capacity for a conscious relationship, finite as we are, with the infinite God. The *likeness* is our dynamic realization of that capacity within the life of ecclesial communion. It is our mirroring of God's beauty, holiness and love in our mind and will. And because God has no limit, we shall continue to grow into the likeness of God for all eternity.

---

[37]Nellas, *Deification in Christ,* 28; John Zizioulas, *Being as Communion,* 55.

[38]Yannaras, *Elements of Faith: An Introduction to Orthodox Theology* (Edinburgh: T&T Clark, 1991), 54–55.

chapter four

THE TRANSFIGURATION
OF THE BELIEVER

N ear the summit of Mount Athos at around 6,000 feet there is a chapel dedicated to the Transfiguration. Each year, before the feast day on August 6th, a party of monks climbs the mountain laden with tools and materials to repair the damage caused by the storms and lightning strikes of the previous winter. The monks then spend the night in the chapel, keeping the vigil of the feast. The next day they return to their monasteries elated, the words of the night office still ringing in their ears:

> Thou wast transfigured upon Mount Tabor, O Jesus, and a shining cloud, spread out like a tent, covered the apostles with Thy glory. Whereupon their gaze fell to the ground, for they could not bear to look upon the brightness of the unapproachable glory of Thy face, O Saviour Christ, our God who art without beginning. Do Thou, who then hast shone upon them with Thy light, give light now to our souls.[1]

---

[1]*Festal Menaion*, trans. Mother Mary and Archimandrite Kallistos Ware (London: Faber and Faber 1969), 478.

The emphasis of the canon is on *theophany*, on the revelation of the divinity of Christ on Mount Tabor and our response to it. It picks out just one strand—though the most important one—of an extremely rich patristic tradition on the Transfiguration. Before we examine these different strands, we must look briefly at how the tradition as a whole developed.

The Transfiguration in the Gospels and the Fathers

We have different accounts of the Transfiguration in each of the three synoptic Gospels. Only John fails to tell the story, perhaps because he conceives of his whole Gospel as a manifestation of divine glory: "And the Word became flesh," he says in his Prologue, "and dwelt among us, full of grace and truth; we have beheld his glory, glory as of the only Son from the Father" (Jn 1.14). For all four Gospels the manifestation of Christ's glory has a central place.

The earliest of the synoptic accounts of the Transfiguration, that of Mark, has been convincingly analyzed by Father John McGuckin.[2] By comparing Mark with Matthew and Luke, McGuckin is able to draw some inferences about the most primitive version of the Transfiguration story and how each of the evangelists has adapted it to emphasize his own theological themes. It appears the pre-Markan version may have been concerned to draw a comparison between Jesus on the "high mountain" and Moses on Mount Sinai. Matthew preserves this primitive aspect when he describes the face of Jesus as shining like the sun and the apostles as filled with awe (Mt 17.1–8)—clearly alluding to Moses with his face

[2]McGuckin, *The Transfiguration of Christ in Scripture and Tradition* (Lewiston/Queenston: Edwin Mellen, 1986), 23–31.

shining with the *shekinah* of God and the Israelites afraid to come near him (Exod. 29.30; cf. 2 Cor 3.7). If this was the case, the two figures seen with Jesus would originally have been angels, as is suggested by the expression "two men" that still survives in Luke's version (Lk 9.30, 32). Mark moves away from this parallelism. He exalts Jesus' status, saying that he was "transfigured" (*metamorphōthē*) before the disciples (Mk 9.2), and calls the two figures seen with him Elijah and Moses, perhaps mentioning Elijah first because at his death he had ascended to God on the *merkabah* throne-chariot (4 Kg 2.1–12) whereas Moses had simply died and been buried (Deut 34.5–6). Jesus is not to be thought of merely as a new Moses. He is the manifestation of God himself, as the voice from the cloud makes clear. The presence of Moses in a supportive role, secondary even to Elijah, emphasizes this.

Matthew follows Mark in using the unusual late Greek work *metamorphoō*, to "transform" or "transfigure," but Luke avoids it. To the latter's more classically attuned ear this might have suggested a god disguising himself. He prefers to speak instead of the appearance of Jesus' countenance as being "altered," and is the only evangelist to use the word "glory" (*doxa*) in this context (Lk 9.29, 31). He is also the only evangelist to mention that Jesus and the three apostles went up the mountain specifically to pray, a detail that was to inspire a rich spiritual tradition among the Fathers.

Each of the evangelists therefore develops different aspects of the episode but all emphasize that the experience of Peter and his companions on the mountain was of theophany, a manifestation of God. In the immediately preceding section Jesus had asked: "Who do men say that I am?" and had received Peter's confession: "You are the Christ" (Mk 8.29; cf. Mt 16.16, Lk 9.20). The Transfiguration fills out the implications of that reply. The Christ is not a new Elijah or a new Moses radiant with a borrowed glory. He is the manifestation of the living God himself.

The Fathers build on this conviction, drawing out the implications of the highly compressed details given by the evangelists. They asked questions about the nature of the experience. Did Christ really undergo any change, or did the change actually take place in the beholders? What was the connection between prayer and the experience of divine light? They suggested ingenious explanations for the differences of detail in the three accounts, such as the timing of the episode, "after six days" in Matthew (17.1) and Mark (9.2), and "after eight days" in Luke (9.28). And they pondered what the Transfiguration indicated about the life of the world to come.

The most important figure in this development is that of Origen. It was he who identified the "high mountain" with Tabor, and who said that Moses and Elijah represented the Law and the prophets. It was he who linked the Transfiguration to the Passion, seeing the radiant garments of Christ as symbolizing the words of Scripture, which only take on their full meaning when seen in the light of Christ's death and resurrection. And it was he too who set in motion the long tradition of seeing the spiritual life as the climbing of a mountain through prayer and asceticism, in order to experience at the summit a transformative vision of God.

Although Origen laid the foundations for all subsequent interpretations, he did not connect the Transfiguration specifically with theosis. The first to do this was the early Byzantine hymn writer, St Andrew of Crete (c. 660–740). For him the Transfiguration is the revelation of the deified humanity of Christ, and by extension, once we have been fully conformed to Christ, of our own deified humanity as well:

> This is clear from the fact that he took chosen apostles with him who were already closer than the others in intimacy, and led them up the high mountain. What was he doing? What was he teaching? He was showing the radiance of his own godhead that transcends all brightness. A little earlier he had done this more mystically but now he does it quite evidently in the Transfiguration, refashioning that nature of which we had heard: "Dust you are and unto dust you shall return" (Gen 3.19). And so, today we celebrate the feast, the deification of our nature, its transformation to a better condition, its rapture and ascent from natural realities to those which are above nature. (*Homily* 7.1; trans. McGuckin)

For St Andrew the Transfiguration symbolizes our passing beyond the limitations of our mortal nature through divine action. There the matter rested until the fourteenth century, when the hesychast controversy suddenly brought the Transfiguration under consideration again.

The hesychast controversy, which broke out between St Gregory Palamas and an Italiote Greek called Barlaam of Calabria in 1340, was about the nature of our experience of God in prayer. Palamas was concerned to defend the reality of the encounter with God of those monks who reported seeing a vision of light at the culmination of intense periods of prayer. In order to establish the nature of this light—whether spiritual or material, created or uncreated—Palamas returns again and again to the Gospel accounts of the Transfiguration. He maintains that yes, the light which the apostles saw was symbolic, but that does not mean that it had no reality. Symbols can work on more than one level. The Taboric light—the light that radiated from Christ—is what Palamas calls an *enhypostatic* symbol, that is to say, something which is a symbol but at the same time is also that which it symbolizes. As symbol, it is accessible to the senses, but as more-than-symbol it transcends human perception. Thus the light is not a created phenomenon. Seeing it enables the beholder to participate in divinity itself. For the light is nothing less than the uncreated radiance of God—a divine energy accessible to the senses in contrast to the divine essence which always remains beyond our grasp. The opponents of hesychasm, by reducing this immaterial and everlasting light to our own mundane level, are guilty of Christological error. The light radiating from Christ cannot be a created light, for this would make Christ less than God.

The debates about the nature of the uncreated light took theological language to the limits of what it is capable of expressing. In order to communicate their teaching more effectively, the hesychasts also made use of visual images. As Andreas Andreopoulos has said in his fine study on the subject, "The icon of the Transfiguration had a role that the written word could not perform: the Transfiguration of the Lord on Thabor was primarily a visual event."[3] Before we examine the theological aspects of the Transfiguration in more detail, we need to look at the iconographical tradition that both interpreted these aspects and influenced them.

---

[3]Andreas Andreopoulos, *Metamorphosis: The Transfiguration in Byzantine Theology and Iconography* (Crestwood, NY: St Vladimir's Seminary Press, 2005), 71.

The Transfiguration in iconography

The oldest surviving representation of the Transfiguration is in the apse of the sixth-century monastery of St Catherine at the foot of Mount Sinai. Here we see a bearded Christ in white and gold garments standing, with his right hand raised in benediction, within a blue mandorla (an almond-shaped background) against a gold ground. Eight rays emanate from him, the two lateral ones touching the standing figures of Elijah and Moses on either side of him, the three lower ones reaching down to John, Peter and James, who are depicted kneeling or lying down.

The mosaic was made in about 560, in the age of the Emperor Justinian. At the time a controversy was raging about how the divine and human natures should be thought of as relating to each other. Here in the mosaic we have an astonishing representation of a human figure shot through with divinity. The interpretation of the human and the divine without separation or confusion is rendered visually in a way scarcely attainable in a written text. What is also remarkable is how the human figures participate in the divine glory. There is a smooth transition from the radiant, almost dematerialized figure of Christ to the serene figures of Elijah and Moses alongside him, and then to the agitated figures of the apostles at his feet. The status of each may be different, but all are grouped around Christ on a gold background. As Andreopoulos remarks, the "transfigured" part is not divided from the "struggling" part as in later icons: "Theosis seems more achievable here than in later depictions."[4]

In later icons there is a marked contrast between the craggy surface of the mountain on which the apostles are depicted in various atti-

[4]Ibid., 138.

tudes of striving and the serene summit where Moses and Elijah are
bathed in the divine light emanating from the transfigured Christ.
The emphasis is on the ascetic struggle that human beings need to
undergo in order to see God. But the effect is not to distance them
from the goal. The viewer is placed in the position of the apostles,
sharing in their experience of ascending to God in prayer:

> The icon of the Transfiguration, in a certain sense, repro-
> duces the experience of the apostles for us; it repeats their
> vision of the transfigured Christ conversing with the Old
> Testament prophets—but now we, the viewers, are put in
> the place of the apostles. It is not merely a narrative icon or
> a teaching aid for the stories of the Gospels, such as the icon
> depicting Christ healing Peter's mother-in-law. The icon of
> the Transfiguration encapsulates the full range and power
> of prayer, from the beginning of ascetic ascent to deifica-
> tion—and therefore it facilitates the transfiguration of the
> believer through prayer.[5]

The interaction between the icon and the viewer can affect the
way the details of the Transfiguration narrative are presented
in written texts. Gregory of Sinai, for example, in his homily
on the Transfiguration, describes the apostles in the following
terms: "And astonished in mind and overcome by the divine light,
they fell to the earth, one on his back, the other face downward,
oppressed by the brightness which welled out from the fount of
light."[6] These details, as the editor of the text comments, "derive
not from the Gospels but from the iconographic tradition."[7] But

[5]Ibid., 71–72.

[6]David Balfour, ed. *Saint Gregory the Sinaite*, 31.

[7]Ibid., 31, note 16.

more often it is the texts that have influenced the iconography. Nowhere is this more evident than in the so-called "hesychastic" mandorla.

The "hesychastic" mandorla first appears in the churches of Mistras, the fourteenth-century Byzantine capital of the Peloponnesus, and in manuscripts of the ex-emperor and fervent hesychastic monk, John Cantacuzenos, some time in the 1350s. It consists of a geometric design within the mandorla surrounding Christ, described by Andreopoulos as "two superimposed concave squares—actually a square and a rhombus—inside a circle."[8] This became the dominant type of mandorla in representations of the Transfiguration throughout the Balkans until the sixteenth century. What does it signify? Three possible explanations have been offered. The first is that the three shapes—the circle, the square and the rhombus—superimposed on top of each other indicate the Trinity. This ties in with Gregory Palamas's attempt to harmonize the "six" and "eight" days of the Gospel narratives. St Gregory suggests that the "six" symbolizes the six figures who were visible, while the "eight" adds the two who were invisible but certainly present—the Father and the Holy Spirit. In this case the "hesychast" mandorla would suggest that our deification implies not only communion with the Son but entry into the life of the Trinity itself. The second suggestion sees an octagon in the geometric shapes that recalls the "Ogdoad," the transcendence of the created world on the eighth day, the day of the Resurrection. According to this explanation our deification is perceived as an eschatological event. The final suggestion is that the geometric shapes within the mandorla represent a sacred map of the universe. Here again the significance would be eschatological, Christ

---

[8]Andreopoulos, *Metamorphosis*, 229–230.

transforming not only the believer but also the entire cosmos at the end of time. For the hesychasts the icon of the Transfiguration allowed them to contemplate the fulfillment of the divine economy throughout the created order.

The Transfiguration as theophany

"What does it mean, 'he was transfigured'? It means he allowed a brief glimpse of the Godhead and showed them the indwelling God." This text from St John Chrysostom (*Selections from Various Homilies* 21), which later Fathers, including St Gregory Palamas, liked to quote, sums up the single most important aspect of the Transfiguration. "There is no other place in the entire Bible," as Andreopoulos observes, "where the curtain between the material and the invisible world is completely lifted visually, and there is no other place where the divinity of Christ is witnessed in such a dramatic way."[9] It was not long, however, before the Fathers began to ask themselves whether this lifting of the curtain did not imply a change in the viewer rather than in the reality that was being viewed. No one has expressed this insight better than St Maximus the Confessor.

The vision of the transfigured Christ, in St Maximus's understanding, implies an internal change in those who seek spiritual knowledge. There is a progression, he says, from the beginners' stage, in which Christ appears in the form of a servant (cf. Phil 2.7), to the advanced stage of those who have climbed the high mountain of prayer, in which Christ appears in the form of God (*Cap. Theol.* 2.13). This manifestation of Christ in his divine nature is not experienced as something external to ourselves. It is interiorized

[9]Ibid., 41–42.

through the life of faith. Picking up on points made by Origen, St Maximus goes on to say:

> When the Logos of God becomes manifest and radiant in us, and his face shines like the sun, then His clothes will also look white (cf. Mt 17.2). That is to say, the words of the Gospels will then be clear and distinct, with nothing concealed. And Moses and Elijah—the more spiritual principles of the Law and the prophets—will also be present with Him.[10]

It is only by having Christ radiant within us that we can enter into the truth which even in the Gospels is veiled from ordinary eyes.

In the *Gerontikon*, the sayings and stories of the desert Fathers of the fourth and fifth centuries, we find several accounts of monks transfigured with light. Three of them stand out: Abba Pambo, "whose face shone like lightning," Abba Sisoes, of whom it was said that "when he was about to die, with the fathers sitting near him, his face shone like the sun," and Abba Silvanus, who was seen with his face and body shining like an angel." These texts have been studied with deep insight by Stelios Ramfos, who sees them as presenting us with an image of what it is to be truly human.[11] Pambo, Sisoes and Silvanus were men whose radiance was the product of inward openness. In Ramfos's view, Pambo's "if you have a heart, you can be saved," is one of the most important sayings in the *Gerontikon*. For the heart in this sense is the spiritual expression of the embodied person. It is the meeting-place of God within us. It is where we find freedom of speech before God. The

[10]*Cap. Theol.* 2.14; *Philokalia* ii, 140–141.

[11]Stelios Ramfos, *Like a Pelican in the Wilderness: Reflections on the sayings of the Desert Fathers*, trans. Norman Russell (Brookline, MA: Holy Cross Orthodox Press, 2000), Ch. 23, "Love and the New Humanity."

pure in heart see God, and they become pure in heart through thanksgiving. It is thanksgiving which enables us to see God, not liberation from the body or the subjugation of the will. When the heart is filled with thanksgiving, egoism disappears. And when we are free from egoism, we share in the self-emptying of Christ. It is only by sharing in the naked humiliated Christ (the kenosis of his divinity) that we can come to share in the glorified Christ (the theosis of his humanity). The focus on the heart maintains the unity of body and soul in the course of this sharing. For the body is not shed to enable us to approach God. Ramfos describes the faces of these abbas not as flesh which is transformed but rather as rocks which sometimes allow the beholder to glimpse a radiant light shining through the fissures.

It is not only the fathers of the distant past who have been seen shining with such radiance. A number of witnesses reported the face of Father Sergius Bulgakov becoming a mass of light on his deathbed in Paris in 1944, exactly like Abba Sisoes fifteen centuries earlier. Perhaps the most famous of these occurrences is that of the transfiguration of St Seraphim of Sarov (1759–1833), which was witnessed in the early nineteenth century by Nicholas Motovilov:

> "But how," I asked Father Seraphim, "can I know that I am in the grace of the Holy Spirit? [. . .] I need to understand completely."

> Father Seraphim then took me very firmly by the shoulders and said, "We are both, you and I, in the Spirit of God this moment, my son. Why do you not look at me?"

"I cannot look, Father," I replied, "because great flashes of lightning are springing from your eyes. Your face shines with more light than the sun and my eyes ache from the pain."

"Don't be frightened, friend of God," Father Seraphim said. "You yourself have now become as bright as I am. You are now yourself in the fullness of the Spirit of God: otherwise you would not be able to see me like this. [. . .] Why don't you look at me, my son? Just look, don't be afraid! The Lord is with us!"

At these words, I looked at his face and was seized with an even greater sense of trembling awe. Imagine in the center of the sun, in the most dazzling brilliance of his noontime rays, the face of a man talking to you. You see the movement of his lips, the changing expression of his eyes, you hear his voice, you feel that someone is holding his hands on your shoulders. Yet you do not see his hands or his body, but only a blinding light spreading around for several yards, illuminating with its brilliant sheen both the bank of snow covering the glade and the snowflakes that fall on me and the great Starets. . . .[12]

Here we have a striking illustration of St Maximus's teaching that the Transfiguration becomes an interior experience through faith—interior but not merely psychological or just imagined. It is an experience of the reality of the god-bearing humanity of those who participate in the Holy Spirit.

---

[12]Cited by Andreopoulos, *Metamorphosis*, 20–21 from the trans. by M.-B. Zeldin published in C. Cavarnos, *St Seraphim of Sarov* (Belmont, MA: Institute for Byzantine and Modern Greek Studies 1980), 93–122.

The Vision of God

The Lord himself, in St Matthew's version of the Beatitudes, promises the vision of God to those who have attained inward purity: "Blessed are the pure in heart, for they shall see God" (Mt 5.8). Commentators have pointed out that the inspiration for this Beatitude comes from a passage in the psalms: "Who shall ascend the mountain of the Lord, and who shall stand in his holy place? He that is innocent in his hands and pure in his heart," who belongs to those "who seek the face of the God of Jacob" (Ps 23 [24]. 3–6). The mountain here is Zion, but the psalm also points to the "high mountain" of the Transfiguration. The desire for the vision of God has always been one of the deepest yearnings of both the Jewish and the Christian traditions.

The Fathers give expression to this yearning very early on. "For the glory of God," says Irenaeus, "is a living man, while the life of man is the vision of God."[13] Irenaeus has three degrees of vision: prophetic in the Holy Spirit, figurative in the Logos (whose manifestation of God to Moses on Sinai was brought to fulfillment after his Incarnation on Mount Tabor), and eschatological in the Father. As Lossky has said, "the third stage, the vision of the Father, the vision possessed by the blessed, is expressed in the appearance of Christ transfigured by that light which is the source of the incorruptible life of the age to come."[14]

The vision of God became a central preoccupation of the monastic Fathers. One of the greatest of the early monks, Evagrius of Pontus (346–399) taught that when the mind is purified of all

---

[13]Irenaeus, *Against Heresies* 4.20.7; cited by Lossky, *Vision of God*, 34.

[14]Lossky, *Vision of God*, 35.

material images it can ascend by means of intellectual vision to participate in the highest realities, "like the incorporeal beings who are surrounded by the radiance of the light of divine glory" (*Eulogios* 1.1; trans. Sinkewicz). Not everyone approved of Evagrius's highly intellectual approach, and in the sixth century he was condemned as a heretic. In spite of this, he has always had his monastic admirers, and indeed Makarios of Corinth and Nikodemos of the Holy Mountain included him in the *Philokalia*. He is much appreciated in monastic circles today, though he still has his critics. One writer who dislikes him is Lossky, who thinks, rather unfairly, that Evagrius replaces "the personal encounter with Christ and intimate communion with the living God" with a lifeless intellectualism.

Lossky is much more drawn to the more biblical spirituality of the heart, as found in the *Gerontikon* and more powerfully still in the Homilies of a Syrian contemporary of Evagrius that have come down to us under the name of Macarius of Egypt. For Pseudo-Macarius, the vision of divine glory takes place not "out there" but within the soul that God has prepared to become his throne and dwelling. Such a soul "becomes wholly light, and wholly face, and wholly eye." It is transfigured by the "ineffable beauty of the glory of the light of the face of Christ" who "has mounted it and sat upon it" (*Hom.* 1.2; Collection A, ed. Dörries-Klostermann-Kroeger, trans. Maloney).

The Macarian approach was taken up by the hesychasts who were convinced that "the kingdom of heaven is within us" (cf. Lk 17.21). From the circle of St Symeon the New Theologian we have a text on the methods of prayer which teaches us how to draw the mind down into the heart through the practice of the Jesus Prayer.[15] Gregory Palamas speaks of the heart as the spiritual center of our being. On the level of the senses we may well experience what we take to be visions of the divine but they are just as likely to be delusory. Only within the heart, within the deep self, do we attain to the true vision of God as uncreated light. Modern hesychasts still follow the same path. Archimandrite Sophrony (1896–1991), who was a disciple of St Silouan of the Holy Mountain before founding a monastery at Tolleshunt Knights in England, discusses his own experience of light in his remarkable spiritual testimony:

> As a young man I was much preoccupied with the mysteries of Being, and more than once I felt—I saw—my thinking energy like a light. The world of mental contemplation is essentially a radiant one. Indeed, our mind is an image of the Primal Mind, which is Light. The intellect, concentrated on metaphysical problems, can lose all sense of time and material space, travelling, as it were, beyond their boundaries. In just such a situation my mind would seem to be light. This state of being is naturally accessible to man but later it became clear to me that it differs qualitatively from the event of the manifestation of God in uncreated Light.
>
> Lord, forgive me—I am feared to speak. Heal me, hearten me.
>
> Withdraw not from me.
>
> The Apostles on Mount Tabor were found worthy to enter the realm of Light proceeding from the Father, and hear His voice bearing witness to His beloved Son. But this became

[15]See *Philokalia*, iv. 70–73.

possible for them only after they had confessed the Divinity of Christ (cf. Mt 16.13 ff.).

It has been granted to me to contemplate different kinds of light and lights—the light the artist knows when elated by the beauty of the visible world; the light of philosophical contemplation that develops into mystical experience. Let us even include the "light" of scientific knowledge which is always and inevitably of very relative value. I have been tempted by manifestations of light from hostile spirits. But in my adult years, when I returned to Christ as perfect God, the unoriginate Light shone on me. This wondrous Light, even in the measure vouchsafed to me from on High, eclipsed all else, just as the rising sun eclipses the brightest star.[16]

Such experiences are granted to the few as a foretaste of the world to come. But they can encourage even those of us who merely read of them.

The Transfiguration as the goal of salvation

The Transfiguration is more, however, than an encouragement to persevere in the Christian life. It is a revelation of the true stature of our human nature, a stature which our first parents in the Garden of Eden failed to attain. They listened to the voice of temptation, which suggested to them that they had been forbidden to eat of the tree of knowledge because God jealously wanted to keep them in a state of immaturity: "For God knows that when you eat of it your eyes will be opened, and you will be like God,

---

[16]Archimandrite Sophrony, *We Shall See Him As He Is* (Tolleshunt Knights, Essex: Stavropegic Monastery of St. John the Baptist, 1988), 155–156.

knowing good and evil" (Gen 3.5). But knowledge in itself does not make us like God. Our twentieth-century history has taught us that only too painfully. "Adam," as St John Damascene says, "longed for deification before the proper time" (*Hom. on Transfig.* 16; trans. McGuckin). Knowledge needs to be accompanied by humility, thanksgiving, purity of heart. The glory indicated by the Transfiguration is only to be attained through the self-emptying of the Passion. "It is only through this free *kenosis*," says Metropolitan John Zizioulas, "that the ascetic is led to the light of the Resurrection. The light of Mount Tabor, the light of the Transfiguration, which the Hesychasts claimed to see, was given as a result of participation in the sufferings, the *kenosis* of Christ."[17] We arrive at our true human stature through sharing in the glory of Christ, having first shared in his Passion.

The Church Father who brings out this aspect of the Transfiguration most clearly is St Cyril of Alexandria. In his homily on the Transfiguration (*Various Homilies* 9) he sets the narrative as Luke tells it within the broader pattern of the divine economy. The immediately preceding discussion is of the greatest significance: "If anyone wishes to come after me let him deny himself and take up his cross and follow me. For whoever wishes to save his life will lose it, but whoever shall lose his life for my sake shall find it" (Lk 9.23). "This teaching," St Cyril comments, "is our salvation." It prepares us for heavenly glory through the acceptance of suffering for Christ's sake. The converse is also true: the vision of heavenly glory granted to Peter, James and John prepares them to accept the suffering that is shortly to come upon them. The Lord's statement immediately before the Transfiguration narrative begins is very significant: "There are those who will not taste

---

[17]Zizioulas, *Communion and Otherness*, 305.

death until they see the kingdom of God" (Lk 9.27). Cyril interprets the Transfiguration narrative in the light of this statement. To see the Transfiguration is to see the kingdom of God. The radiant humanity of the Lord shows the apostles the destiny that awaits them. The Lord can now go to his suffering and death and the apostles can follow him, confident in the glory that can only be attained through sharing in the Cross.

There is a further point to be made. The vision of the Transfiguration was a shared experience. As Andreopoulos puts it, "a genuine mystical experience is not intentionally an affair of one."[18] The presence of the three apostles points to the ecclesial dimension of theosis. We cannot attain our full human stature as isolated individuals.

The Transfiguration as the fulfillment of the age to come

Archbishop Anastasios Yannoulatos has described theosis as a fundamental human right, "the right to become that for which we were created."[19] The Transfiguration teaches us that this "becoming" is a journey that passes through suffering to the glory of the deified humanity revealed in Christ. Nobody is a better guide to this journey and its final goal than St Maximus the Confessor. For St Maximus the Transfiguration prefigures the Eighth Day, when, in philosophical terms, we shall enjoy "a face-to-face vision of the self-subsistent forms of goodness, seeing them as they are in themselves" (*Cap. Theol.* 2.17; trans. *Philokalia*), that is to say,

[18]Andreopoulos, *Metamorphosis*, 27.

[19]Anastasios Yannoulatos, *Facing the World: Orthodox Essays on Global Concerns* (Crestwood, New York: St Vladimir's Seminary Press, 2003), 75.

when we shall encounter the ultimate reality that lies behind the goodness of this world—God himself. The Lord has two forms, says St Maximus. The first is a form that can be perceived by the many. This was the form in which he was seen in first-century Palestine, and it is the form in which he is available to us today in texts and visual images. "The second is more hidden, and can be perceived only by a few, that is, by those who have already become like the holy apostles Peter and John, before whom the Lord was transfigured with a glory that overwhelmed the senses" (*Cap. Theol.* 1.97; trans. *Philokalia*). This hidden form is the form seen by St Symeon the New Theologian, St Seraphim of Sarov or St Silouan of the Holy Mountain. It marks the dawning of the Eighth Day even in the present life, for it prefigures, in St Maximus's words, "the second and glorious advent, in which the spirit of the Gospel is apprehended, and which by means of wisdom transfigures and deifies those imbued with spiritual knowledge: because of the transfiguration of the Logos within them 'they reflect with unveiled faces the glory of the Lord'" (2 Cor 3.18) (*Cap. Theol.* 1.97; trans. *Philokalia*). We may not yet have attained to the heights of St Symeon, St Seraphim, or St Silouan, but we can be sure that this humanity transfigured with the glory of the Lord is "that for which we were created."

chapter five
SELF-TRANSCENDENCE

U p to this point we have been considering various theological approaches to theosis that arise out of an understanding of the divine economy. Our focus has been on
biblical texts and themes. We now turn to a more philosophical
approach. This approach, which has its origins in the first attempts
of the Greeks to ponder the nature of reality, was developed by
the Fathers and has become important again as modern Orthodox
thinkers explore what it means to be a human person. We are
not self-contained beings; we cannot be explained—nor can we
exist—without reference to something beyond ourselves. We need
to share in the life of God, not to escape from our humanity but
in order to become more truly human.

Yearning for the "really real"

It is widely accepted that there is more to reality than just our
own conscious selves and the tangible world around us. We seem
to have an inbuilt desire to transcend our humanity, to reach out
to something absolute and enduring that leaves the limitations of
our bodily lives behind.

Reflection on this desire goes right back to antiquity. On a popular level many were fascinated by the powers of the mind, the way it could travel in a flash to distant places, or even soar up to the stars. On the philosophical level it was Plato who first took the transcendence of the human mind seriously. For him the "really real" was something that existed only in the spiritual world. The purpose of philosophy was to enable the mind to grasp this fact and live by it.

There are various modern versions of such an approach. Iris Murdoch, for example, expounded it eloquently in her philosophical work, *The Sovereignty of Good* and, with equal power, though less explicitly, in many of her novels. Some thinkers, however, are suspicious of any aspiration at all to transcend humanity, on the grounds that this would seem to deny that we are finite bodily beings. Self-transcendence appears to them to deprive us of our humanity. Others see transcendence as implying a communion with the divine that far from denying our humanity actually affirms and fulfils it. In this chapter we shall look at how ancient writers discussed the theme of self-transcendence and what some of their modern successors have made of it.

Knowing yourself

One way in which we can discover whatever it is that transcends humanity is by looking within ourselves. This idea, too, goes back to the ancient Greeks. Think of the famous inscription above the entrance to the Temple of Apollo at Delphi, which read: "Know Yourself!" What this meant was much debated in philosophical circles. In Socrates' view, according to Plato, self-knowledge was wisdom, and wisdom was an understanding of the limitations of what we know—a "knowledge of knowledge and ignorance"

(*Charmides* 172b). Happiness consequently lay in self-restraint and in acquiring the knowledge that enabled us to distinguish between good and evil.

By the time Christian thinkers began to grapple with "Know Yourself!" many centuries later, there had been a number of developments. These began with Plato himself. His famous Allegory of the Cave in Book VII of the *Republic* pointed to the existence of a reality beyond what is accessible to the senses. We are like prisoners chained in a cave, facing the back wall. There is a fire behind us near the mouth of the cave, and images passing in front of it cast shadows on the cave wall. In the absence of any other knowledge we take these shadows to be the reality. The object of philosophical effort is to escape from the prison of the cave and, passing beyond the images and the fire, to look upwards into the light. Reality is external to us. There is no inner world to explore. But Plato's concept of intellectual vision was to be fundamental for later thought on the subject of inwardness. No one is more important for this later phase than Plotinus, described by his ancient biographer, Porphyry, as "the philosopher of our times."

According to Plotinus (c. 205–270), we live simultaneously on several different levels. The lowest is that of the body, because of its fragility and transience. Porphyry says that Plotinus "seemed ashamed of being in the body," and reports that he never celebrated his birthday or allowed his portrait to be painted (*Life of Plotinus* 1). This indicates not so much disdain for the body as a focus of interest elsewhere, on contemplation. The true self is within, an object of endless fascination but accessible only to the mind. The lower part of the true self is the *psyche,* the body's animating power. Above the *psyche* is the *nous,* or mind. The point of the philosophical life is to subject the lower part of the soul (the *psyche*) to the higher part (the *nous*). Once this is accomplished the mind can rise to the contemplation of the intelligible world, which is the world of mental objects. Our whole spiritual being thus becomes unified as the thinking mind becomes identical with the object of thought. The lower part of the soul unites with the higher self, the *psyche* becoming fully integrated with the *nous*.

But beyond the world of intelligible reality, or universal mind, there is an ultimate level of reality which Plotinus calls the One. There is a further step available to human beings, which is in union with the One. Plotinus describes this as a dizzying leap into the void, as an ecstatic self-surrender, of which erotic love is but a faint image. It is the overcoming of all duality. Even the concept of "vision" is inadequate because vision still implies duality, the one who sees remaining distinct from the one who is seen. Plotinus uses several analogies to convey what he means. It is like two torches which merge and become one, yet can move apart and are still seen to be two. Or it is like the centers of two circles which are superimposed. The same point becomes the center of both circles until the circles are separated and the one point becomes two again. This ultimate unity is unity with the divine and yet it is not a unity with anything outside ourselves. It is when the self knows itself in a direct and immediate way that it "sees" the divine.

Plotinus was not alone in thinking in this way. He was the greatest philosopher after Plato and Aristotle and drew many other thinkers in his wake. Christians, too, were fired by his vision to express the insights of their faith in similar terms. In the third century, Plotinus' great Christian contemporary, Origen of Alexandria, used to teach his pupils in the early stages of their studies to look into their souls, where they would find reflected an image of the divine mind. To know themselves was to discern something of God. Another Christian contemporary, the author of a *Refutation of all Heresies*, identified by some scholars with Hippolytus of Rome, also says that self-knowledge is equivalent to divine knowledge. There is a reciprocal relationship between God and humanity. To know the God who made us is to have knowledge of ourselves and vice versa.

For Gregory of Nyssa in the fourth century the purified soul becomes a mirror of divine perfection. Through the contemplation of a reality accessible only to the mind, the soul is drawn more and more deeply into the experience of the presence of God. Some writers speak of this as an ascent towards a brilliant light. But Gregory prefers to describe it as an entry into darkness, on the analogy of Moses' entry into the darkness and cloud on Mount Sinai, where he encountered God. Sharing in the divine is a disorienting experience, where we lose all our familiar bearings as we mingle with a reality which is so close as to be almost part of us and yet at the same time utterly transcendent.

Augustine of Hippo, who died in 431, shares in this tradition, developing the later Platonic idea of finding God through looking inwards. But he brings to it a new insight. In his view the soul should be thought of as inner space. We have to enter into this space, for only then can we look up towards God who is above and beyond it. It is within our hearts that we can best discover Christ, whom Augustine identifies with the eternal wisdom sought by the philosophers.[1]

---

[1] This development is usefully explored by Phillip Cary, *Augustine's Invention of the Inner Self* (Oxford and New York: Oxford University Press, 2000).

God, for Augustine, is fundamentally intelligible, i.e., accessible to the mind. He is to be identified with the Plotinian level of universal mind, or *Nous*. But among the Neo-platonists of the Christian Greek world, God is beyond *Nous*. He is to be identified only with the transcendent One. In Dionysius the Areopagite—not St Paul's first Athenian convert, but the sixth-century Syrian author who adopted his name and identity—the level of *Nous* corresponds to the created angelic realm. Augustine, committed to the intelligibility of God, dispenses with the Plotinian One. For him the ultimate divine level is *Nous*. But Dionysius and his Greek successors conceive of God as transcending *Nous*, and therefore as being in his essence inaccessible to the human mind.

These different adaptations of Platonism underlie many of the later controversies between Eastern and Western theologians in the Middle Ages. Broadly speaking, the West understood God as intelligible, the East as beyond intelligibility. This had repercussions on how the believer could participate in God. For Dionysius there could be no union with the One—the hidden reality of God beyond all substance or essence—only with the perceptible radiance of God that reveals his presence. Nor can such union be attained by intellectual effort alone. It requires a going out of the self in ecstasy, a movement of love that is reciprocated by God as he himself goes out in ecstasy to meet the believer.

For St Maximus the Confessor love is also primary. This love is a mystery. It expresses both a natural yearning of the soul for union with God and a reciprocal condescension of God to the soul that has made itself receptive. Through love, the human and the divine converge. God and humankind are drawn together in a single embrace. Theosis is thus a sharing in the divine attribute of eternity. It is not an excellence attainable only by a spiritual elite. It is the goal for which humanity was created.

Some modern writers have represented Maximus as holding an almost Buddhist concept of God.[2] This is to misread his teaching on divine transcendence. God cannot be known in his essential being, but he *has* manifested himself in his incarnate Word. In the person of Christ we can know the Father and the Spirit. Through the Son's hypostatic union with the flesh, the Father and the Spirit have become accessible to humankind. The Father is therefore not a transcendent void beyond human cognition, because we do have access to him in Christ. Consequently, self-transcendence is achieved not by losing ourselves in a non-personal ultimate reality and thus attaining the wisdom of emptiness (noble as that may be), but by assimilating ourselves to Christ.

Maximus presents this idea in a number of different ways. At his most philosophical he can indeed sound as if we lose our identity in the overwhelming vastness of God. In the *Ambigua*, his most profound work, he speaks of our recovery of divine unity in terms of our transcending the five divisions that permeate the whole of reality. These, in ascending order, are:

- male/female (the fundamental division in all bodily life)

- paradise/the inhabited world (the division between the spiritual and the mundane)

- heaven/earth (the division between the eternal and the temporal)

[2]For example, Karen Armstrong, *A History of God* (London: Heinemann, 1993), 155.

- intelligible reality/sensible reality (the division between what is accessible to the mind and what is accessible to the senses)

- uncreated nature/created nature (the division between God and everything that is not God)

As we rise through these levels, we come to realize that the whole of creation is "wholly interpenetrated by God." Finally, we lose all sense of apartness from either creation or God, becoming "completely what God is except on the level of being" (*Ambigua* 41, 138B). Yet we do not give up our humanity. Our self-transcendence does not annihilate us. For the overcoming of these divisions is only achieved by healing and perfecting our human nature in Christ.

The way we come to be "in Christ" is through encountering him personally in the Gospels and in the Mysteries (or Sacraments) of the Church. When St Maximus speaks of our feeding on the Word as the bread of life, he means it in two senses. We receive him as our intellectual food in the sacred text and as our physical food in the holy Eucharist. Through these receptions we make our own the new humanity represented in Christ's person, a humanity perfectly united with God.

We thus transcend our fallen humanity by becoming the body of Christ. It is through participating in Christ intellectually, ascetically and liturgically, in mind and body, that we receive the gift of theosis. For we do not posses the potentiality for it by nature.

The experience of ecstasy

In his *Ambigua* Maximus speculates on the nature of the Apostle Paul's famous claim to have been caught up to the third heaven (2 Cor 12.1–5). For Maximus this third heaven is largely symbolic. He suggests that it could refer to a third way of knowing God, a mystical way complementing what he calls "practical philosophy" (which is the ascetic life) and "natural contemplation" (which is the investigation of the principles that make things what they are). Or it could refer to Paul's perfect love, the third great virtue surpassing faith and hope. These suggestions do not preclude a literal understanding of Paul's ecstasy, for Maximus also believes that when the Apostle was rapt out of the body, he received a supernatural initiation that transcended words and knowledge (*Ambigua* 20, 1240B–1241B).

Paul's is the earliest Christian mention of a mystical ascent to heaven. But it is not an isolated testimony. It belongs to a tradition which was well established in Judaism, and provides us with a vivid pictorial alternative to the highly intellectual Neoplatonic version of the experience of attaining union with God. The tradition begins with the prophet Ezekiel, who at the beginning of his career describes his vision of the awesome throne-chariot of God, called the *merkabah* (Ez. 1.1–28). It continues with Jewish apocalyptic writings, such as the non-canonical Book of Enoch, in which the eponymous hero is carried off from the world in a whirlwind and set at the end of the heavens, where he sees the dwelling places of the holy and the Elect One of God (Enoch 39.3–7). And it is found among the early desert fathers, who were avid readers of apocalyptic books and themselves describe visionary journeys to heaven. Abba Poemen, for example (4th cent.), once fell into an ecstasy, and on being pressed by another monk to tell him where he had been, said that he had stood with the Mother of God weeping at the foot of the Cross (*Apophthegmata*, Poemen 144). Abba Silvanus (4th cent.), on being questioned in similar circumstances, said that he had been seized up to the Judgment and had seen many monks going to hell while people leading a life in the world entered the kingdom of heaven (*Apophthegmata*, Silvanus 2). And St Antony the Great (4th cent.), on returning from an ecstasy in a state of intense grief, was forced to explain that he had witnessed the sufferings of the wrath to come (*Life* 82).

In the later monastic tradition such apocalyptic visions recede, and ecstasies come to be connected more with the vision of light. St John Climacus (7th cent.), while occasionally mentioning the alarming side of ecstasy, also regards it as the highest form of prayer:

> The beginning of prayer is the expulsion of distractions from the very start by a single thought; the middle stage is the concentration on what is being said or thought; its conclusion is rapture in the Lord. (*Ladder*, Step 28)

St John sometimes experienced ecstasy himself, as did St Symeon the New Theologian (10th cent.). St Symeon introduces a further refinement. He makes a distinction between the sudden ecstasy that sometimes comes to the beginner and the unceasing ecstatic prayer of the perfect. In modern times St Silouan of the Holy Mountain experienced an ecstasy, clearly of St Symeon's first kind, when he was still a young novice. According to his biographer, Archimandrite Sophrony, it occurred during Vespers at the Russian monastery of St Panteleimon in the church of the Holy

Prophet Elijah, where "to the right of the royal gates, by the icon of the Saviour, he saw the living Christ." Archimandrite Sophrony comments:

> From his words and from his writings we know that a great divine light shone about him, that he was taken out of this world and transported in spirit to heaven, where he heard ineffable words; that he received, as it were, a new birth from on high.[3]

The light that St Silouan experienced is a characteristic feature of the hesychastic tradition. In the fourteenth century the precise nature of this experience became a matter of intense theological debate. The defenders of hesychasm maintained that it signified a participation in the uncreated energies of God leading to deification, while its opponents argued that the experience was a created effect brought about in the believer by the operation of grace. Hesychast teaching was vindicated by several church synods in the mid-fourteenth century, and the official statements that they produced are still normative for Orthodox spirituality today. Modern Orthodox writers on self-transcendence acknowledge the importance of these statements, but since the middle of the last century have been influenced by another powerful current, that of personalist philosophy.

Modern Orthodox personalism

Personalist philosophy springs from the conviction that personality is a spiritual and ethical category which gives meaning to human existence. It was popularized in the Orthodox world by

---

[3]Sophrony, *St Silouan the Athonite*, 26.

---

the Russian thinker Nicolas Berdyaev, who makes a sharp distinction between the person and the individual. Individuality, in his view, belongs to the natural order, while personality expresses freedom and the spirit. Human personality is not subordinate to any other value. It is an end in itself. And it is affirmed by the exercise of freedom. Mere individuals are in servitude to the state and to society. But persons are free, unique and unrepeatable, because they bear within them the image of God. The self-realization of personality moves the person away from the objectification that makes it a part of nature and therefore enslaves it. It "gives actual effect to the divine idea of man."[4] Through realizing our personhood, we transcend the limitations of being a part of nature, and as we thus bring out the image of God within us, we express the supremacy of freedom.

Vladimir Lossky, a younger contemporary of Berdyaev, makes use of these ideas in his teaching that we grow towards personhood by participating through the Holy Spirit in the divine energies. But it is the Greek professor, Christos Yannaras, who develops them most fully in a series of works spanning nearly three decades from *On the Absence and Unknowability of God* (1966; Eng. trans. 2006) to *Postmodern Metaphysics* (1993; Eng. trans. 2004). Yannaras identifies true being with participation. Participation in what? In an ultimate otherness that is *personal*. This ultimate personal otherness is what we call God. But God in himself is beyond human participation and knowledge. So how do we experience the participation that is required if we are to become true beings, or persons? By a relationship that Yannaras characterizes as erotic and ecstatic. By these terms (which he draws ultimately

[4]Berdyaev, *The Beginning and the End* (London: Geoffrey Bles, 1952), 136.

from Dionysius the Areopagite) he means a going out of ourselves in self-transcendence and self-offering. The very existence of God is ec-static. Inaccessible to us in his essence, God goes out to us in his energies, actively summoning us to a personal relationship with him. This does not mean that the energies are some kind of impersonal force. They can only be experienced in the persons of the Trinity. "The fulfillment of God's ecstatic, erotic movement to human kind," says Yannaras, "is the Incarnation of the Word."[5] And the model for our response is Christ's own loving communion with his Father, which we can only share in through the experience of participation in a living communion with him that is found in the Church. Christ's mode of existence (participation in the fullness of life) is the mode of existence for our new human nature. The result of God's consummating movement towards us and of our own erotic, ecstatic response to him, is our theosis, our coming to exist in the mode of God without identity of essence. This is the ultimate meaning of self-transcendence.

John Zizioulas is close to Yannaras in his approach but more theological than philosophical in his emphasis. He starts from a fundamental conviction, namely, that we are not self-sufficient simply as human individuals but have a yearning for communion with something, or rather, someone, beyond ourselves. It is the fulfillment of this yearning which brings us to personhood. But to commune with another created being like ourselves is not sufficient to satisfy our longing. Only uncreated being can satisfy us, because only communion with the uncreated can enable us to transcend the boundaries of our creaturely existence and over-

[5]Christos Yannaras, *On the Absence and Unknowability of God: Heidegger and the Areopagite* (London/New York: T&T Clark International, 2005), 108.

come death. The concepts Zizioulas uses to express this are those of *ecstasy* and *hypostasis*. It is only by going out of ourselves (by an ecstatic movement) that we attain personal existence (by a hypostatic, or "really existing," union) as partakers of the divine. God is necessary to our personhood. Without a transcendent personal being beyond ourselves there is no basis for our relational existence as persons.

These modern thinkers develop several philosophical strands of tradition in the Greek Fathers which seek to explain how finite human beings can attain communion with a God who is personal yet also infinite and supremely transcendent. Building especially on Dionysius the Areopagite and Maximus the Confessor, they argue that by responding to God in love and self-offering we can transcend the limitations of our finite existence because God himself reaches out to us in eros and ecstasy.

chapter six

PARTICIPATION IN
THE DIVINE LIFE

"Participation" seems a straightforward word. The *Oxford English Dictionary* defines it as "the fact or condition of sharing with others." But among the Fathers and more recent Orthodox writers it implies something rather more complex. In its Greek form, "participation" (*methexis*, *metousia*, or *metochē*) is a philosophical term with both a weak and a strong sense. In the weak sense it means "sharing in the attributes of another." In the strong sense it is used to account for whatever has no being in its own right, whatever is not self-caused: things exist "by participation" when they depend on something else. They have no identity conceivable entirely in itself.

The New Testament

In our examination of 2 Peter 1.4 ("partakers of the divine nature") we saw how the sense of "partakers" (in this instance *koinōnoi*) moved from the weak form in the New Testament author (sharing in the divine attributes of glory, goodness and incorruption) to the strong form in Cyril of Alexandria (human nature transformed in Christ). This may be thought of as a transition from a philosophical idea of participation to a theological understanding of the attainment of true personhood through incorporation into Christ.

This strong form of participation draws on St Paul's teaching on the believer's participatory union with Christ. Our being "in Christ," as he puts it, through baptism and the life of faith is one of the Apostle's central themes.

> Do you not know that all of us who have been baptized into Christ Jesus were baptized into his death? Therefore we have been buried with him by baptism into death, so that, just as Christ was raised from the dead by the glory of the Father, so we too might walk in newness of life. For if we have been united with him in a death like his, we will certainly be united with him in a resurrection like his. (Rom. 6.3–5, New RSV)

By clothing ourselves in Christ through the agency of the Spirit, we acquire a new identity which enables us to live with the life of Christ, sharing in his Cross so that we may come to share in his glory. This mystical identification with Christ makes it possible for us to share in his relation with the Father, calling him "Abba, Father!" just as he himself does (cf. Rom. 8.15; Gal. 4.6). Our solidarity in Christ that is initiated by baptism is continued and perfected by our participation in the Eucharist:

> The cup of blessing that we bless, is it not a sharing in the blood of Christ? The bread that we break, is it not a sharing in the body of Christ? Because there is one bread, we who are many are one body, for we all partake of the one bread. (1 Cor 10.16–17, New RSV)

The change in us brought about by participation in the new creation through baptism is confirmed and consolidated by the sharing of the Eucharistic body and blood of Christ. In Paul's teaching, participation in Christ lies at the very core of salvation.

The patristic age

The first to make "participation" an essential element of his theological thinking was the great third-century Alexandrian, Origen. Origen introduced a distinction between a participation in God which is natural, which belongs to the structure of our being, and one which is supernatural, which belongs to our growth in the spiritual life. The first kind is a product of reason and refers to the fact that we owe our existence to a cause outside ourselves. It is to do with our status as contingent beings dependent on that which is Being in an absolute sense. The second kind is a product of revelation and refers to the fact that that which is being in an absolute sense is personal. This personal being is not locked in its oneness but is threefold and is not static but reaches out to us, actively transforming us.[1] The Holy Spirit sanctifies those who respond in faith, making them partakers of the Son, who by giving them a share of his divinity raises them to the right hand of the Father. Our becoming partakers of the divine nature signifies our sharing in the divine attributes of the Son, not through our own efforts but through the initiative of the Holy Spirit.

Origen's insights were taken up in different ways by Gregory of Nyssa and Cyril of Alexandria. Gregory worked out a theory

[1]Origen first works this out in the first and fourth books of *On First Principles* and in the second book of the *Commentary on John*. For a detailed discussion with references, see my *Doctrine of Deification*, 147–152.

of the soul's ascent to God which has been very influential. He speaks about three different stages or "ways" in the spiritual life: the way of light, which is the purificatory stage, the way of the cloud, which is the contemplation of spiritual reality, and the way of darkness, which is entered when the soul begins to reflect the perfection of God. These stages are based on the account in Exodus of Moses' ascent of Mount Sinai to meet God, passing through the cloud to the summit of the mountain wrapped in smoke (Exod. 19.16–20). The last stage, the way of darkness, is attained by participation. This is to participate in nothing less than God, to possess in a created mode, as Andrew Louth has put it, what God is in an uncreated mode.[2] Such participation through ascent to the divine darkness restores the image of God in us. But this is not called "deification" in Gregory's terminology. "Deification" is a word he reserves for the operation of Christ in the sacraments. Baptism enables us to transcend our human nature by becoming sons and daughters of God. It prepares us for Christ's mingling of himself with our bodies in the Eucharist, uniting our mortal flesh to what is immortal so that we might participate even corporeally in his incorruption.

Cyril's approach is focused more strongly on participation, not simply in the divine attributes, as in Origen and Gregory, but in the new life which the incarnate Word inaugurated. He retains Origen's distinction between a natural and a supernatural participation. On the natural (or ontological) level we are as dependent for our being on God as heat is on the fire that radiates it, or as fragrance is on the flower that exudes it. Just as the heat and the fragrance are distinct from their source but have no existence

[2]Louth, *The Origins of the Christian Mystical Tradition* (Oxford: Oxford University Press, 1981), 92.

without it, so our created being is distinct from the uncaused being of God but is impossible without it. On the supernatural level Cyril is thoroughly Christocentric. Our dynamic participation in the divine life is accomplished within the context of the Church's mysteries. Commenting on the Lord's words in St John's Gospel, "Unless you eat the flesh of the Son of man and drink his blood, you do not have eternal life in you" (Jn 6.53), Cyril declares:

> For those who do not receive Jesus through the sacrament will continue to remain utterly bereft of any share in the life of holiness and blessedness and without any taste of it whatsoever. For he is Life by nature, seeing that he was born of a living Father. And his holy body is no less life-giving, for it has been constituted in some way and ineffably united with the Word that gives life to all things. (*Comm. on John* 4.2, 361ab)

The flesh of Christ has been deified by its union with the Word. The Eucharist will therefore "certainly transform those who partake of it and endow them with its own proper good, that is, immortality." The mechanics of such a transformation are beyond human comprehension. Yet Cyril offers some analogies to help us understand:

> Do not be astonished at this, or ask yourself . . . about the "how." Instead, reflect on the fact that water is cold by nature, but when it is poured into a kettle and put on the fire, it all but forgets its own nature and moves across to the energy of that which has dominated it. In the same way, although we are corruptible because of the nature of the flesh, we too through our mingling with Life abandon our own weakness

and are transformed into its property, that is to say, into life. For it was absolutely necessary, not only that our soul should be re-created into newness of life by the Holy Spirit, but also that this coarse and earthly body should be sanctified by a coarser but analogous participation and be called to incorruption. (*Comm. on John* 4.2, 362ab)

Our participation in Christ through the Eucharist is both corporeal and spiritual. The spiritual aspect is supported and strengthened by the Holy Spirit. For because the Spirit is God, when we receive him we become partakers of God. With regard to the divine being, the Spirit is "from the essence of God," but with regard to the economy he is "of the Father and the Son" (*Comm. on John* 9.1, 809d). He works always in unison with the Son to sanctify and spiritualize, that by making us partakers through him of the divine nature he might enable us fully to realize our sonship in Christ and thus have access to the Father. In other words, Cyril relies on the idea of participation to express a dynamic relationship with the Father that is *though* the Spirit and *in* the Son, which he sums up by quoting Paul: "Because you are sons, God has sent the Spirit of his Son into your hearts, crying, 'Abba! Father!' " (Gal. 4.6).

In the earlier Byzantine theologians "participation" is used uncontroversially to express a sharing in the divine attributes ("Theosis", says Dionysius, "is participation in one-like perfection" [*Ecclesiastical Hierarchy* 66.2.18, 376A]), and in particular to emphasize the dependent and secondary nature of such sharing ("I become totally god," says Symeon the New Theologian, "not in essence but by participation" [*Hymn* 50.201–202]). In the fourteenth century, however, participation became a matter of dispute as a result of Gregory Palamas's theory of deification through participation in the divine energies. Debate arose over how we can know God. Gregory's first opponent, Barlaam the Calabrian, held that by intellectual analysis of the phenomenal world we can come to know God indirectly as the ultimate cause of all that exists. But Gregory himself was not impressed by the powers of human reasoning. His approach was purely religious: "the fear of the Lord is the beginning of wisdom." This calls for a life of prayer and asceticism. The fruits of such a life are the nurturing of divine love, the goal of which is illumination by God and participation in the divine life.

But how can we participate in God? Gregory's opponents (drawing on Dionysius the Areopagite) held that God was beyond human knowledge—beyond being itself. We can, however, participate in his attributes of goodness and oneness. For Gregory this was far from satisfactory. His experience of hesychastic prayer had taught him that we can, if God himself grants it, participate in him in a far more intimate way. We can share in the source of divine life itself. To explain how this could be possible he developed the distinction between the essence and the energies of God which is hinted at in the Cappadocian Fathers and worked out more fully by Maximus the Confessor. There are divine realities, or powers, in which created beings can participate. Such realities cannot therefore be the essence of God, yet are still in a real sense divine. These Gregory calls the energies. Their divinity is not derivative, that is to say, they do not exist "by participation." Nor are they distinct from God, like a fourth person of the Trinity, as his opponents claimed. The whole of God is present in each of his energies. And those who participate in them participate in the whole of God. Theosis is a gift of the Spirit, communicated through participation in the Spirit's deifying energy. This gift is not something apart from God and therefore created. It is the Spirit himself in his mode of self-giving. Theosis therefore expresses a *relation*, not a thing. Through theosis we become *homotheoi*, one with God, not because we have become what God is in his essence, but because we have come to share in his attributes. Unlike Dionysius, however, Gregory does not go so far as to say that we can share in the oneness of God: we share only in his plural aspects.

Modern Orthodox theologians

Modern Orthodox theologians have for the most part followed St Gregory's lead. In the remainder of this chapter we shall look at three representative figures, Vladimir Lossky, Christos Yannaras and John Zizioulas. The first two of these regard the essence/energies distinction as fundamental to Orthodox theology, while the last has expressed certain reservations.

Lossky was deeply committed to the essence/energies distinction, which he held to have been present in Orthodox theology from the beginning. For him this distinction expressed the truth that God was simultaneously both supremely transcendent and fully immanent in the world. The essence and the energies are simply two different modes of God's existence: "God reveals Himself, totally gives himself in His energies, and remains totally unknowable and incommunicable in His essence."[3] There is a paradox here which calls for some discussion.

In his dialogue *Theophanes* Palamas had argued that we must hold that we both share and do not share in the divine nature (*Theophanes* 15). We have to maintain both positions. When

---

[3]Lossky, *In the Image and Likeness of God*, 55.

challenged to explain how this can be so, he embarks on a defense of the reality of divine-human communion: we are not absorbed into the divine nature yet it is our destiny to partake in it in such a way that we become possessed solely by the divine energy (*Theophanes* 16). This holding together of two apparently contradictory ideas is what Lossky calls an antinomy. He believes that such antinomies are vital if we are to protect the real character of our communion with God.

The essence/energies distinction, however, has seemed to many to run into serious logical difficulties. First, it appears to divide God into two parts, producing, besides the persons of the Trinity, a fourth hypostasis, as Palamas' opponents claimed. Secondly, if God fills the whole of creation with his energies which are equally God, it becomes difficult to avoid the charge of pantheism. The dilemma has been put by Aristotle Papanikolaou in the form of the following syllogism: "If the energies are God, then everything is God. If everything is not God, then the energies are less than God." Papanikolaou himself does not find this argument compelling, but neither is he entirely comfortable with the logic of the Palamite position. He goes on to say:

> It would be incorrect to characterize the essence/energies distinction as illogical, for the paradoxical nature of the distinction is grounded in the paradoxical event of divine-human communion. It does seem, however, to violate a basic principle of logic, the law of non-contradiction.[4]

The law of non-contradiction did not worry Lossky. In fact he saw an exaggerated concern for logical neatness and consistency

[4]Papanikolaou, *Being With God: Trinity, Apophaticism, and Divine-Human Communion* (Notre Dame, IN: University of Notre Dame Press, 2006), 27.

as one of the main weaknesses of Western theology. Antinomic theology, in his view, "which proceeds by oppositions of contrary but equally true propositions,"[5] is indispensable if we are not to diminish divine truth: "The goal of this antinomic theology is not to forge a system of concepts, but to serve as a support for the human spirit in the contemplation of divine mysteries."[6] For the human spirit really does experience God, and it does this by participating in divine attributes which are not just "abstract concepts applicable to the divine essence, but living and personal forces."[7]

It is the personal aspect of these forces that has fired the imagination of a Greek thinker much influenced by Lossky, Christos Yannaras. For Yannaras, the distinction between the essence and the energies is the starting-point of all knowledge about God. We can know nothing about God as he is in himself. We can only know him through the mode of being by which he makes himself accessible to us experientially. That is to say, we can only know him through his energies. Knowledge implies participation. We can only know in a real sense that in which we can share in some way. As essence, God can only be an object of rational enquiry, the final cause of all that is. But if he is nothing more than essence, "*theosis*, the participation of human beings in the divine life, is ultimately impossible."[8] The experience of the saints teaches us that it is indeed possible to know God in an intimate and personal sense. And it was to defend the reality of such experience that the essence/energies distinction was pronounced Orthodox by the Constantinopolitan synods of the mid-fourteenth century.

[5]Lossky, *Image and Likeness*, 51.

[6]Ibid., 52.

[7]Ibid., 57.

[8]Yannaras, *Person and Eros*, 65.

Yannaras preserves the antinomy that Lossky regards as so important. *What God is* is beyond our capacity of knowing. But *who he is* is made accessible to us in a mode of being we can know "by participation."

> Thus, the divine energies call to an experience of *participation* with the *imparticipable* Godhead, and this conceptual contradiction (of participation in the imparticipable) constitutes a real (unique) possibility of knowledge with reference to the accessibility of the reality of God.[9]

Yannaras's antinomic theology enables him to maintain that God is utterly transcendent and yet at the same time personal: "The divine energies reveal to us the *personal* existence and otherness of the living God—they make the Person of God accessible to human experience, without abolishing the inconceivable abyss of the *essential* distance that separates us from God,"[10] As to how the divine energies reveal the personal existence of God, Yannaras offers a human analogy. When we listen to a piece of music by a great composer, Mozart for example, even if we have not heard the piece before we can often identify it as his work. The piece is not simply in the style of Mozart, it *is* Mozart. In the listening to the music we encounter the mind of the composer by participating in his creative act. We have a relationship with Mozart himself, with his personal uniqueness and otherness.[11]

---

[9]Yannaras, *On the Absence and Unknowability of God,* 87.

[10]Ibid., 85.

[11]Ibid., 115–115. He develops this analogy more fully in his *Postmodern Metaphysics* (Brookline, MA: Holy Cross Orthodox Press, 2004), 113–114; 153; 179–180.

The analogy, of course, only takes us so far. It helps us to understand how we can say that we do not just know *about* God, we know him by experience through sharing in his divine being. But it tells us nothing about the triadic nature of God or about the significance of the Incarnation. The question therefore arises that if the energies, as an invitation to loving relationship, take us directly to a personal encounter with God, what is the role of Christ? Yannaras is very clear about two things, (a) that the essence of God does not exist outside the divine hypostases or persons—"each person recapitulates and expresses the whole *mode of being*, complete divinity or humanity"[12]—and (b) that the second person of the Trinity became incarnate, maintaining the unity of divine life and the hiddenness of the divine essence while at the same time manifesting to us a new mode of existence that unites God with humanity. This new mode of existence, incarnate in Christ, is a life of complete communion of the divine and the human natures. As such, it restores to us the possibility of participation in the life of God. As Yannaras puts it, it is "now up to the freedom of each person to be attuned existentially . . . with the *mode of existence* of the 'new' theanthropic nature of Christ."[13] It is our free response that brings us into the body of the Church. The Church is the context in which the individual becomes a person, in which an impoverished autonomy becomes an existential unity with one another and with God. Seen in this light, the Church is the "communion of persons that participate in the very experience of life."[14] This, then, is the kernel of theo-

[12]Ibid., 87.

[13]Ibid., 92.

[14]Ibid., 96.

sis—participation in the divine energies through communion with Christ in his body which is the Church.

Turning now to John Zizioulas, we find that he does not define theosis in terms of participating in the divine energies. In fact, he does not use the term "participation" (*methexis*) very much at all, preferring "communion" (*koinōnia*) instead. Unlike Lossky, Yannaras and most other Orthodox theologians, he has serious reservations about the whole concept of the energies. Palamas' teaching seems to him to make the energies "an *ontological* notion"—to give them a reality apart from the divine being. For him the energies are not to be maximized: "it is ultimately *personhood*, the *hypostasis* of the *Logos,* and not divine energies, that bridges the gulf between God and the world."[15] His idea of theosis is therefore centered on the concept of personhood, not on participation in the energies.

Zizioulas describes God's revelation of his name, "I am that I am" (Exod 3.14) as "the ultimate ontological claim," indicating that God is "the only being that is in an ultimate sense 'itself'."[16] The being of God is "itself" in a different way from our own being. Our sense of our own particularity carries with it an awareness of our boundaries. God, being infinite, has no boundaries. His personhood—that of the Father, for it is the Father who is God in an unqualified sense as "the ultimate ontological principle of divine personhood"[17]—is expressed by *ekstasis,* which is an ecstatic going out of himself in communion with the Son and the Spirit.

---

[15]*Communion and Otherness,* 30.

[16]Ibid., 215.

[17]Ibid., 130.

Human personhood does not become complete until it becomes an image of God, in the sense of replicating this going out of the self in communion. Theosis, as the goal of salvation, thus requires that "the personal life which is realized in God should also be realized on the level of human existence."[18]

The model and means of our realizing true personhood by going out of ourselves in communion with the Other is the incarnate hypostasis of the Logos, Jesus Christ. Zizioulas, following a strand of patristic tradition prominent in Irenaeus, Cyril of Alexandria and Maximus the Confessor, identifies theosis with adoption, not with participation.[19] It is by being incorporated into the new humanity hypostasized in the Son that we become by grace what he is by nature, sharing through the Spirit in his communion with the Father. Theosis is realized at the level of hypostasis, not at the level of energy. And the hypostasis of the Son, as defined by the Council of Chalcedon, is the key to our understanding how theosis is structured. Zizioulas focuses on two key adverbs defining the union of the two natures in Christ: *asynchytōs* ("without confusion") and *adiairetōs* ("without division"). The first implies divergence, the second convergence; the first safeguards freedom, the second love.[20] For freedom is the maintenance of diversity, while love is the impetus towards union. Thus in Christ "the *created* and the *uncreated* are perfectly united without their specificities being abolished."[21] And this theanthropic unity-in-diversity becomes the model for the ultimate fulfillment of our own per-

---

[18]*Being as Communion*, 50.

[19]*Communion and Otherness*, 30–31, note 51.

[20]Ibid., 260.

[21]Ibid., 261–262.

sonhood, not by nature but by grace, through our experience of the Church.

The liturgical life of the Church makes manifest among us a mode of being reflecting that of Christ, a mode of being which expresses love in its fullness without destroying our freedom or specific identity. In the relationship of eucharistic communion love and freedom come together to realize our true personhood. All identity, whether biological or social, arises from a network of relationships. Our Christian identity in its most complete sense is created by the relationship of ecclesial communion experienced in the Eucharist. "There is no *theosis* outside the Eucharist," says Zizioulas, "for it is only there that communion and otherness coincide and reach their fullness."[22]

Yannaras and Zizioulas represent two different approaches to participation in God, each of which is the fruit of profound meditation on different strands of the patristic tradition. Yannaras locates theosis on the level of the divine energies, Zizioulas on the level of the hypostases. Yannaras speaks of participation in the energies, Zizioulas of communion through the Eucharist. The approaches are different but complementary. We shall return to them in the next chapters.

---

[22]Ibid., 85.

---

chapter seven
UNION WITH GOD

"**H**oly Father, keep them in thy name, which thou hast given me, that they may be one, even as we are one" (Jn 17.11). In his great high-priestly prayer as he prepares to embark on his Passion, the Lord prays that his disciples may become "one thing"—*hen* in the neuter—just as the Father and the Son are "one thing." The nature of this "one thing" is explained by St Cyril of Alexandria:

> He wishes them to be bound together tightly with an unbreakable bond of love, that they may advance to such a degree of unity that their freely chosen association might even become an image of the natural unity that is conceived to exist between the Father and the Son. (*Comm. on John* 17.11, 972b)

The disciples are to attain a oneness in unity of *will* on analogy with the natural oneness that exists between the Father and the Son. Analogy is not the same as identity. We all share in the same human nature but "identity of substance in our case is not of the same kind as that which exists in the case of the Father and God the Word who is from him" (*Comm. on John* 17.11, 972d). True Christians may be perfectly united with each other, but there is no sense as yet of their aspiring to union with God. As modern commentators have pointed out, the word "union" (henōsis) is not used in the New Testament or the Septuagint. The most that Cyril will say is that we become gods by participation in the Holy Spirit, that when we come to share in the divine life through having the Spirit dwelling within us, we will enjoy a derivative mode of being rooted in God—not by nature but by grace.

Union with God in the Greek Fathers

It is in the early sixth-century writings of St Dionysius the Areopagite that we first hear a Church Father speaking about *union* with God. St Dionysius defines theosis, it may be remembered, as the attaining of likeness to God and union (henōsis) with him (*Ecclesiastical Hierarchy* 1.3.376A). Likeness and union are two aspects of the same goal, which is to be achieved by our returning to the source of our being and thus realizing our highest selves. The bold image which St Dionysius uses to convey this idea comes from the experience of ecstatic love. Union with God is the product of divine *eros*, as the lover strives to be united with the object of his or her longing:

> Lay aside the faculties of the senses and reach up, so far as possible, without the use of discursive reasoning to union with him who transcends all being and knowledge. For shedding all things, you will, by a wholly unqualified and absolute ecstasy that detaches you from all things, be lifted up to the ray of the divine darkness. (*Mystical Theology* 1.1,997B–1000A)

God is beyond being. Yet paradoxically the goal of the spiritual life is becoming one with him. How is union possible between two such radically different levels of reality? The answer is through *ecstasy*, a going out of the self under the impulse of love, to which God responds by going out himself in ecstasy to meet the lover. The union with God which the soul achieves is thus not with his hidden transcendence, but with the perceptible radiance by which he goes out of himself to reveal his presence to us, as he did to the disciples on Mount Tabor.

This is heady stuff! It could easily be pushed to unorthodox extremes, which is precisely what happened within a few decades of the Dionysian writings in a Syriac text called *The Book of the Holy Hierotheos*. The subject of this work is the ascent of the mind to God. But Hierotheos, the supposed teacher of St Dionysius, does not stop at a union simply with the radiance of God. The mind, he teaches, must rise above all duality and "commingle" with the Universal Essence itself. It must transcend even love, for love implies two opposite poles: the lover and the beloved. "When it has passed beyond every duality, even beyond unification, when all distinction is removed, it reaches its fulfillment—the summit of its ascent—which is complete identity with the Good" (*Hierotheos* 4.18–21).

The correction to such teaching is supplied by St Maximus the Confessor. When St Maximus speaks of our recovery of divine unity, he does so in terms of our gradually overcoming all divisions, first those of our created world, beginning with the division between male and female, and finally even the division between created and uncreated nature. We become *what* God is—not, as in Hierotheos's teaching, *who* God is—in every way except on the level of being. Which means that while remaining, as we do, still on our human level, yet with nothing separating us from God, we attain the perfect likeness of God. This is possible through our participation in that divine mode of being by which God makes himself accessible to us. What St Dionysius calls the divine "powers" (*dynameis*) are transformed by St Maximus into the divine "energies" (*energeiai*).

The hesychast tradition follows St Maximus's interpretation of St Dionysius. We become the same as God but different, a unity-in-diversity through participating in the divine energies. For St Symeon the New Theologian this is expressed on the one hand by the vision of the divine light, and on the other by union with Christ through receiving him in the Eucharist. These are not "two ways," two alternative approaches. As Bishop Hilarion Alfeyev observes, Symeon "presupposes that the Holy Spirit should be 'manifested' in the one who has partaken of the Eucharist . . . The stress is placed on mystical illumination by the divine light through Communion."[1] In the words of one of St Symeon's own hymns:

> Purified by repentance
> And by floods of tears,
> Partaking of the divinized body,
> As of God Himself,
> I myself become a god
> By this unspeakable union.
> (*Hymn* 30.467–472; trans Alfeyev)

Niketas Stethatos, St Symeon's disciple and biographer, provides us with a theoretical account of how such union is achieved. He speaks of three stages, based on St Dionysius' three stages of purification, illumination, and perfection. The first is through the prac-

[1]*St Symeon the New Theologian*, 90–92.

tice of the virtues to attain spiritual knowledge of created things. The second is through contemplation to perceive the essence of created things. And the third, the goal of all contemplative activity, is to become "interfused with the primordial light." These three levels of contemplation correspond to ascending degrees of union. The first brings us into unity with ourselves. The second joins us in the union of love with all others who are wounded by a divine longing for God. The third inducts us "—wholly irradiated by the Spirit—to the unity of God Himself"[2]

The fourteenth-century hesychasts teach a similar threefold ascent. For St Gregory of Sinai, "a divine philosopher is he who through ascetic purification and noetic contemplation has achieved a direct union with God" (*On Commandments and Doctrines* 127, *Philokalia* iv. 246). St Gregory Palamas introduces a further subtlety. For him we attain unity with God when we replicate within ourselves God's three-in-oneness: "When the intellect's oneness becomes threefold, yet remains single, then it is united with the divine Triadic Unity." St Gregory looks inwards to find God. His threefold approach expresses an insight into the mind's reflex character, its ability to turn back on itself. The three-in-oneness that the mind can attain is to be "both the guard, that which is guarded, and that which prays while it is keeping guard" (*Three Texts on Prayer and Purity of Heart* 2, *Philokalia* iv. 344). As St Gregory says, it is difficult to persevere in this for any length of time. But those who can do so, and are deemed worthy, will be united to God—not to God in his essence, for the essence of God is imparticipable, but to the uncreated divine energies through the operation of the Holy Spirit.

[2]*On Spiritual Knowledge* 31–37, 47–48; trans. *Philokalia* iv. 148–149, 153.

Approaches to union with God in modern Orthodox thinkers

The Byzantine approach to union with God through ascetic discipline, eucharistic communion and contemplative ascent has remained normative to the present day, especially in the context of monastic life. But alongside this approach others have arisen, mostly centered on speculation about the nature of the human person. These new approaches were opened up by Russian theologians and religious philosophers, who came to the West after the Bolshevik Revolution of 1917. In recent years thinkers from other Orthodox traditions have developed them further.

The Russian ideas go back to the great nineteenth-century theologians, Alexis Khomyakov (1804–1860) and Vladimir Soloviev (1853–1900). In the early part of the twentieth century they received powerful expression in the writings of Sergius Bulgakov (1874—1948) and Vladimir Lossky (1903–1958). The first two of these provoked a considerable amount of opposition in official Church circles. The third, while supported by his bishop, Metropolitan Evlogy, also attracted criticism.

Bulgakov is perhaps best known for his controversial notion of sophiology. This is based on the conviction that the world is related to God through divine wisdom, or Sophia, which is bringing all things gradually to their intended goal in God:

> Only in the light of Sophiology can we grasp all the scope of that eschatological fulfilment of all things, which is not limited to the final separation of good and evil in the last judgement, but transcends even that separation, for then God shall be all in all and Divine Wisdom fulfilled in the created.[3]

[3]Bulgakov, *The Wisdom of God*, 217 cited by N. Zernov, *The Russian Reli-*

All matter is potentially holy, and human beings have a unique role to play in realizing that holiness in cooperation with the divine Creator. "God created the world," says Bulgakov, "only in order that he might deify it."[4] Such deification is brought about by sophianization:

> a union with God that has already been accomplished for all of creation through the union of two natures, divine and human, in Christ, according to the Chalcedonian dogma, and through the descent of the Holy Spirit upon the apostles and all of humankind, according to the dogma of the Pentecost.[5]

Two inferences may be drawn from this statement. First, because the union was accomplished in Christ, it must be of a *personal* character. Which implies that our own attainment by grace of divine-human life can only take place through personal communion with Christ. Secondly, because the union is also the work of the Holy Spirit descending upon humankind, it must involve our free cooperation. Which implies the Orthodox doctrine of synergism, namely, that "human energy necessarily participates in the work of salvation, that is, in the assimilation of deification, even if the degree of this participation is diminished by original sin."[6] Hence the importance of prayer, which, as Bulgakov says, is not only "an essentially *personal* relation," but is also an expression

gious Renaissance in the Twentieth Century (London: Darton, Longman and Todd, 1963), 297.

[4]Bulgakov, *Wisdom of God*, 203; cited by Zernov, *Russian Religious Renaissance*, 296.

[5]Bulgakov, *Bride of the Lamb*, 203.

[6]Ibid., 306.

of human freedom.[7] Through prayer we receive grace. This "is not something special that is offered to man outside the Incarnation and Pentecost. Rather, it is the gift of the Incarnation and Pentecost."[8] Grace is thus a mode of being which is personal, which respects our freedom, and which links us to the hypostatic source of life. It is a mode of being summed up in the word "love," an ever-deepening oneness with God which nevertheless does not abolish the distinction between the lover and the beloved:

> Its goal is the perfect deification of humankind, when God will be all in all. But it does not have an end, since deification is *eternal* life in God, which is inexhaustible and without end for ages of ages. But this eternal life in God always retains its initial premises: not only the difference between the Creator and creation, the unpassable distance between them, but also the freely synergistic relation between them. Creation is not abolished, is not consumed by divine fire, does not drown in the ocean of the divine depths, is not annihilated before God's magnificence. It remains in its creaturely identity, for it is posited to being by God and it itself posits itself to being in its freedom. That is the mystery of createdness, God's love for creation, to which creation responds with its own ardent love for God. This is the reciprocity of the love of God and creation, which is also a "synergism."[9]

Personhood, freedom and love are also central to Berdyaev's thought: "Whenever one of these elements is absent, then Chris-

[7]Ibid., 309.

[8]Ibid., 305.

[9]Ibid., 308.

tian mysticism suffers thereby."[10] Berdyaev identifies two fundamental tendencies in mystical thought, one monistic the other dualistic. Monism deifies the world in such a way as to make it identical with God, turning the world itself into a divine principle. Dualism creates an unbridgeable gulf between God and the world, turning the material creation into an objective thing that we can use and exploit. Christian mysticism, or more specifically theosis, is neither monistic nor dualistic, "neither a monistic identity with God nor a humiliation of man and the created world. Theosis makes man Divine while at the same time preserving his human nature."[11] Monism and dualism are reconciled through what Berdyaev calls "a dialogical and dramatic relationship" between God and humanity made possible by the *personal* nature of Christian spirituality.[12] This third way is based on the theandric mystery of Christ, the God-manhood revealed to us in the Incarnation. Christ is both divinity in its fullness and humanity in its fullness, expressed personally and therefore characterized by love: "There is no love without personality, for love is a radiation from one personality to another."[13] By sharing in divine love through Christ, we become spirit and thus attain true freedom.

Berdyaev is dissatisfied with mysticism understood simply in terms of contemplation. Contemplation, in his view, is far too passive a state. A dynamic process of change is vital, otherwise contemplation becomes "an eternal, hermetic and finite circle of being immune from external intervention and complete in itself." The

[10]Berdyaev, *Spirit and Reality* (London: Geoffrey Bles, 1939), 147.

[11]Ibid., 149.

[12]Ibid., 148–149.

[13]Ibid., 147.

human being must not be a passive contemplator. "Only when he frees himself from the objectification of concepts, from the notion of static being, does man begin to understand the essentially active and creative nature of the relation between man and God."[14] Our relation to God must be an active response to the divine summons, not a passive contemplation of the Divine. Passivity leads to the objectification of the spirit: "Spirit is betrayed and transformed into a conventional symbolism," as Berdyaev puts it, making idols of the nation, the Church and so on. "Real spiritualization is a process of subjectification; it involves an order based on subjectivity, on the existential subject, a personalistic order."[15] This subjectivity has nothing to do with self-centeredness. The sin of egocentricity is to treat all things that are not ourselves as objects. True subjectivity releases the divine element in us. Berdyaev saw this as ushering in a new spirituality in his own age.

Lossky was a vigorous opponent of Bulgakov's sophiology, and like many of the émigré Russians regarded Berdyaev as a maverick. Nevertheless he follows in the footsteps of his older contemporaries in many ways, agreeing with Berdyaev on the importance of the person, while insisting with Bulgakov that "union with God cannot take place outside of prayer."[16] It is his conviction that union with God is the perfection of the personal character of a human being. This means that it cannot take place in a private way; it calls for an ecclesial identity as an essential prerequisite:

> All the conditions necessary for attaining this final end are given to Christians in the Church. But union with God is

[14]Ibid., 173.

[15]Ibid., 189.

[16]Lossky, *Mystical Theology*, 206.

not the result of an organic or unconscious process: it is accomplished in persons by the co-operation of the Holy Spirit and our freedom ... The personal character of a human being who has entered on the way of union is never impaired, even though he renounces his own will and natural inclinations.[17]

Union with God is the final stage of theosis, an ascent by action (the overcoming of the passions) and contemplation (the grasping of the spiritual realities). It is the product of turning to God in repentance and prayer, of cooperating with him by a synergistic harmony of wills, of dwelling in ecstasy in the divine glory. It is best attained by the path of hesychasm, which is the focusing of the whole of one's attention inwards through the practice of the Jesus Prayer. It was through calling on the Name of Jesus that the anonymous author of *The Way of a Pilgrim* was overwhelmed with bliss and discovered the meaning of the words: "the Kingdom of God is within you." By commending hesychasm, Lossky brought back into theological discourse the distinction between the essence and the energies of God. After him no Orthodox theologian could speak about the way of union without taking the divine energies into account.

Lossky was not alone in his rediscovery of hesychasm. In Romania Father Dumitru Stăniloae published a major study on St Gregory Palamas in 1938. At about the same time he began his work on the *Philokalia*, enlarging the original Greek version and adding his comments to it. His work on *Orthodox Spirituality*, which summarizes hesychast teaching, appeared in 1981. This book was based on the lectures on mystical theology he gave at the

[17]Ibid., 216–217.

Theological Institute of Bucharest. (The un-Orthodox sounding title was because the Communist censors at the time did not like the word "mysticism" but would allow "spirituality.") Stăniloae opens the third part of the work, which is on "Perfection by Union or Deification," with the same statement that we find in Lossky's chapter on "The Way of Union" in his *Mystical Theology*: "Union with God can only be reached by pure prayer." Both of them are drawing on St Gregory Palamas. But Stăniloae goes further than Lossky in almost merging the believer with God. Commenting on a passage from St Gregory on the way the mind can transcend prayer though ecstasy, he says that union is not strictly speaking prayer itself "because in prayer the consciousness of the distinction with God is still too clear."[18] But it *is* the product of prayer: a mutual interpenetration which floods the mind and the body with divine love.

Stăniloae was imprisoned by the Communist authorities for five years from 1958 to 1964 at a time when Romanian Christians were being treated with particular harshness. Some time afterwards, on being asked what prison had taught him, he replied: "I realised that our theology had been too abstract and theoretical ..."[19] In *Orthodox Spirituality* he gives an experiential account of "spirituality." Union with God is the product of an ecstasy of love, "the sentiment that forms with God a 'we.'" Perpetual ecstasy is possible only in the life to come. But in this life we can emancipate the self, not by loving our fellow human beings so that we can love God, but the other way round: "We have the feeling that in the love of God as ecstasy, God has opened His heart to

[18]Stăniloae, *Orthodox Spirituality*, 304.

[19]Obituary by A. M. Allchin in *Sobornost* 16.1 (1994), 40.

us and received us in it, just as we have opened our heart so that He can enter it."[20] The mind—or rather the heart, the core of our human person—is penetrated wholly by God without being confused with him. Always anxious not to be merely abstract and theoretical, Stăniloae offers a comparison from human experience: "when I see you in a moment of ecstasy of love, I see myself in you too."[21] This is the mutual indwelling of humankind and God, with us in God and God in us:

> So all will be in God and we will see all things in Him . . . and the unitary presence of God in all things will be real to the extent that all creatures gathered in Him remain real and unmingled in God. This is the eternal perspective of deification.[22]

It was not until 1964 that Lossky's *Mystical Theology* was translated into Greek. Christos Yannaras has called this "one of the most influential Orthodox books of the twentieth century."[23] In Greece it contributed to the creation of a new theological outlook and the naturalization of a new—or perhaps the recovery of an old—theological vocabulary. In the same year Yannaras left Greece to pursue postgraduate studies in France and Germany, where he encountered the thought of Heidegger and the French existentialists. This encounter stimulated him to go back to the Fathers, particularly to St Dionysius the Areopagite and the Fathers of the hesychast tradition, and re-express their teachings in a philo-

---

[20]Stăniloae, *Orthodox Spirituality*, vol. i, 325.

[21]Ibid., 337.

[22]Ibid., 374.

[23]Christos Yannaras, *Orthodoxy and the West* (Brookline, MA: Holy Cross Orthodox Press, 2006), 292.

sophical language which he hoped would be better able to communicate with people today. The result was a remarkable series of books which on the topic of union with God reaches its most complete expression in *Person and Eros* (4th edition 1987).

The fundamental insight of *Person and Eros* is that personhood is relational. We do not exist as little islands of being complete in ourselves: "We know the person only in the fact of relation."[24] Relationship defines what we are, our *hypostasis*. The fullness of personal existence is *hypostatic*. Yannaras defines this in technical language in the following way: " 'Hypostasis' signifies the dynamic reality and wholeness of personal existence in its ecstatic mutual *perichoresis* and total communion, the antithesis of the distantiality of atomic self-containedness."[25] This means that to be persons in the full sense we need to be in communion with other people and with God. As isolated individuals we may think we are independent and self-reliant, but our humanity is in fact crippled.

So how is this relational existence expressed? The answer is through the Dionysian categories of ecstasy and eros. Ecstasy means literally a "standing out." It refers to the possibility of going out of ourselves, of transcending ourselves, through responding to God's erotic call or summons to participate in the divine life. "Erotic" in this context does not refer to sexuality, except insofar as it is a metaphor drawn from human experience. It refers to our potentiality for total communion with God and the intensity of our yearning for it. Eros expressed in ecstasy defines us as persons. It signifies a transcendence of the limitations of individual self-

[24]Yannaras, *Person and Eros*, 250.

[25]Ibid., 255.

containedness, a new mode of existence to which we are called. But for this to take place, God also needs to go out of himself. As Yannaras puts it, again in more technical language:

> This mode of existence, which indicates the fullness of personal otherness without impairing the unity of the nature, is revealed in the referential ecstasy of God outside his nature, in the summons to communion and relation which the personal God addresses to the personal human being.[26]

To speak of God going out of himself in ecstasy implies some kind of duality in God, some sense in which he reaches out to humanity and makes himself accessible to us and yet at the same time remains utterly transcendent and inaccessible in his essential being. This duality is expressed by the distinction between the divine essence and the divine energies. The "ecstasy" of God in his divine energies is how God "stands out" from himself, "offering himself as the potentiality for total personal communion."[27]

When we speak about personal communion between human beings, we are speaking about the communion of like with like. How do we relate in a personal manner to a being of a different order of reality from ourselves? How does a human being, in Yannaras's words, have "a personal potentiality to *be-opposite* the divine personal existence"?[28] There is no possibility at all of this happening if all there is is the divine essence and human existence. The Triadic energy of God summons us to the realization of a relation *outside of* the divine nature. Our "logical" constitu-

[26]Ibid., 253.

[27]Ibid., 258.

[28]Ibid., 261.

tion as human beings suggests this—we are "a 'combination' and 'union' of *logoi* [inner spiritual principles] revelatory of the divine energy." We "embody the divine summons to the realization of a relation with God outside of the divine essence."[29] Human beings, in effect, recapitulate in their own persons the whole of what in essence is outside of God.

But our actual experience is rather of the fragmentation of human nature and of our distance from God. This is what the Fall represents, which we make personally our own when we refuse the divine summons to communion with God: "The free refusal of personal participation in this natural union with the Godhead perpetuates the 'unnatural' mode of existence of the Fall, which is humanity's hell."[30] Our choice in fact is between a personal going out towards God (*ec-stasy*), by which we attain union with him in his divine energies, or a falling away from God (*apo-stasy*) by which we become increasingly fragmented parts of a merely natural world.

Hell is the torment of not loving, as Dostoevsky says. It is remaining locked into our self-contained individuality, unable to go out of ourselves in ecstasy or to attain relation and communion. Hell is destroyed in the person of Christ, for the Incarnation is the definitive uniting of human nature with divine nature. Christ makes possible the restoration of personal communion with the Godhead by giving us access to a new mode of existence.

We experience the restoration of this personal communion through grace, a term Yannaras helpfully defines:

[29]Ibid., 261.

[30]Ibid., 271.

The grace of God is not some indeterminate kind of divine "blessing" which is added quantitatively to humanity's natural capabilities. It is the life-giving summons and ground of the summons ceaselessly issued by God for humanity to participate in the existential fulfillment of personal communion with the Godhead.[31]

Grace is not a "thing" we receive. It is God of his own free will meeting us in ecstasy. It restores us to our integrity and wholeness, making us complete persons.

Personhood is thus attained within the Church. The Church is defined by Yannaras as "a 'gathering together of those previously scattered' atomic individuals of fragmented nature into the unity of loving perichoresis and existential communion with God."[32] The Church is where through Christ "the inability of nature to realize an ecstatic relation of communion with the Godhead has been definitively lifted. The human person is no longer condemned to remain within the existential limits of natural individuality."[33] This arrival at complete personhood is "the conclusion of our moral journey, the attainment of theosis or deification, the goal towards which the Church strives."[34]

Like Christos Yannaras, John Zizioulas is noted for his "personalist" approach to divine-human relations. In an essay of 1975, reprinted in his *Communion and Otherness* (2006), he describes the human person as fundamentally relational: "the person can-

[31]Ibid., 289.

[32]Ibid., 270.

[33]Ibid., 270.

[34]Ibid., 293.

not be conceived in itself as a static entity, but only as it *relates to*."[35] Personhood implies "openness of being," that is, "a movement towards communion which leads to a transcendence of the boundaries of the 'self' and thus to *freedom*."[36] This is what constitutes the person's "ecstatic" character. The person is also "hypostatic," in the sense that each of us exists in a mode which is unique and unrepeatable. Our uniqueness is established in free communion with others. "That which, therefore, makes a particular personal being be itself—and thus be at all—is, in the final analysis, *communion, freedom* and *love*."[37]

So far Zizioulas sounds very much like Yannaras. But he disagrees with him on a number of points. In a study published originally in Greek in 1978 and subsequently in a revised English version in 1985, he challenges Yannaras's use of Heidegger as a way into the thought of the Greek Fathers.[38] Zizioulas acknowledges that Heidegger can liberate theological thought, as Yannaras believes, from philosophical rationalism, but points out two major difficulties. First, Heidegger's ontology (his theory of being) makes all being, even the being of God, subject to time. Secondly, Heidegger's identification of being with the *revelation* of being makes the divine economy, the mode of God's revelation in time, "the starting point and the *ontological structure* of the theology of the Holy Trinity." Zizioulas admits that Yannaras attempts to advance beyond Heidegger by identifying ecstasy not "simply

[35]Zizioulas, *Communion and Otherness*, 212.

[36]Ibid., 213.

[37]Ibid., 214.

[38]Zizioulas, 'Personhood and Being' in *Being as Communion*, note 40, pp. 44–46.

with the *mode* by which whatever exists *appears* to emerge on the horizon of time" but "with the experience of personal catholicity, that is, of ecstatic, erotic self-transcendence."[39] Nevertheless, he is not convinced that Yannaras has overcome the difficulty of using Heidegger for the interpretation of patristic theology.

Zizioulas's own priority is, like the Cappadocian Fathers, to maintain the "monarchy" of the Father—that is to say, the Father as the principle and source of divine being. The three persons of the Trinity are not all on the same level, as they would be if, in Heideggerian terms, they had a parallel existence on a common "horizon" of disclosure. There is an ontological *structure* in the theology of the Trinity. This has implications for how we attain communion with God. Not through participation in the divine energies (about which, as we have seen, Zizioulas has reservations) but through participation in the body of Christ. Zizioulas is for this reason more Christological in his emphasis than Yannaras. "Man 'in Christ' becomes a true person *not through another 'schesis'* but only in and through the one filial relationship which constituted Christ's being."[40] Christ is the model for our own humanity in a structural rather than a moral sense. In him the dialectic of created and uncreated "is raised to the level of personhood." This means that communion with God is for us "a dialectic of *difference* and not of division." What we attain is God in a unity-in-diversity.

> Thus, man becomes truly man, that is, he acquires fully his natural identity in relation to God, only if he is united with God—the mystery of personhood is what makes this possi-

[39]Ibid., 45.

[40]Zizioulas, *Communion and Otherness*, 239.

ble. *Theosis*, as a way of describing this unity in personhood, is, therefore, just the opposite of a divinization in which human nature ceases to be what it really is.[41]

Christ is the model for a humanity which is not individualized and fragmented. He is the model of true personhood, a personhood in which we can begin to participate through being baptized in the Spirit into Christ. In this sense every baptized person can *become* Christ, can attain that mode of being in which nature exists in its ecstatic movement of communion. Everyone can "put on" Christ, in St Paul's words, or, in Zizioulas's terminology, can attain personhood, a state in which the distantiality of individuals is turned into the communion of persons.

The restoration of true personhood in Christ through baptism has ecclesial and eucharistic implications. If Christ is understood primarily as an individual, the result is "either a mysticism of some kind of erotic union with Christ the individual, or a sacramental-eucharistic mysticism centred on the objectified eucharistic body."[42] The body of Christ is "the community of the 'many' in the realization of man's unity with God."[43] "Spiritual mysticism," Zizioulas insists, "is always ecclesial and passes through the community; it is never an individual possession."[44] The Eucharist is "the mystical experience of the Church *par excellence*." It is "a vision of glory of a transfigured creation."[45] Zizioulas objects to the ascetic fathers being called the mystical theologians *par excel-*

[41]Ibid., 243.

[42]Ibid., 294.

[43]Ibid., 294.

[44]Ibid., 295.

[45]Ibid., 297.

lence. Granted, they do teach us how to attain freedom through breaking down our egocentric will. But eucharistic or ecclesial mysticism has a different emphasis. It presupposes the theandric Christology of Chalcedon,

> according to which union between man and God is realized in Christ without division but at the same time without confusion, that is, a perfect unity which does not destroy but affirms otherness. The Church as the "mystical body" of Christ is the place where this Christologically understood "mystical union" is realized.[46]

Our union with God is thus not a private psychological experience but can only be achieved within the eucharistic body of the Church.

The thinking of the authors we have been considering affirms in a variety of ways the reality of divine-human communion. As such it has been very influential. But it has also provoked criticism. In the 1930s Bulgakov's sophiology was attacked by serious Russian theologians such as Lossky as an unfortunate innovation owing more to nineteenth-century German philosophy than to the Orthodox theological tradition.[47] Some of Bulgakov's lesser critics even accused him of trying to make Sophia a fourth member of the Trinity. The latter charge was plainly absurd. Bulgakov saw sophiology as a fresh approach to speaking about grace. He wanted to avoid any language that seemed to turn grace into a "thing" simply added on to nature. The creaturely Sophia is God's power in creation, "the divine image in man, who is the micro-

[46]Ibid., 307.

[47]Lossky, *Spor o Sofii* [The Controversy about Sophia] (Paris: Confrérie de Saint Photios, 1936).

cosm linking all of creation with God."[48] Sophianicity is therefore creation's capacity for God:

> In its sophianicity, creation contains the image, or imprint, of the divine principle of its being. Creation awaits and thirsts for the fullness of its proto-image, its "glory," which is given in the action of grace. Thus, the distinction between natural and supernatural grace expresses, in reality, the relation between the Divine and the creaturely Sophia, between divinity and the world in the process of its deification.[49]

Bulgakov contrasts this with a Latin theology which presupposes an unbridgeable chasm between God and creation. In the classic Thomist scheme two kinds of grace are required, one created, the other uncreated, in order to supply a middle term linking God and the world. In Bulgakov's scheme, grace is divine humanity itself in the process of being accomplished:

> Man's capacity for participating in the divine is the divine image, which is the very foundation of his being. This image is an unceasing call to deification, to the actualization of the power of Divine-humanity, to the sophianization of life, to the identification of the Divine and the creaturely Sophia. The identification has already been realized in the Church, which is the body of Christ and the temple of the Holy Spirit, the life in Christ by the Holy Spirit, the revelation of the Holy Trinity. This is the inexhaustible source of the grace-bestowing power of deification, which leads man from glory to glory.[50]

[48] *Bride of the Lamb*, 295.

[49] Ibid., 296

[50] Ibid., 300.

These ideas received their fullest expression in the final volume of Bulgakov's great trilogy on Divine Wisdom and Godmanhood, *The Bride of the Lamb*, which was published posthumously in Russian in 1945.[51] Although Bulgakov was not personally censured, his sophiology caused unease in official ecclesiastical circles. On its original publication in Russian *The Bride of the Lamb* was received with some suspicion. It was nearly forty years before a French translation appeared. And only at the beginning of this century has it become available in English.

More recently, criticism has focused on the work of Yannaras and Zizioulas. In 1985 the university professors Savvas Agouridis and John Panagopoulos published long articles in the journal *Synaxi* in which they attacked what they saw as an alien intrusion into Orthodox theology of philosophical existentialism and personalism.[52] Agouridis denounced Yannaras and Zizioulas for ignoring the historical and social dynamic of the Christian message in favor of a theoretical individualism. Panagopoulos, in a more considered essay, argued that the assertion that person precedes essence is unfounded. Person and essence, he insists, cannot be distinguished logically or in time from each other. The personal character of Christ's human nature lies in the fact that it receives and manifests the fullness of the Triadic Godhead—Christ's human nature is personal because it is theanthropic: the human and the divine interpenetrate each other. The realization of our own personhood takes place through the *imitation* of Christ. The

---

[51]This volume is on Creation and the Church. The other two volumes, *The Lamb of God* (on Christ) and *The Comforter* (on the Holy Spirit) were published in 1933 and 1936 respectively.

[52]These articles are analyzed by Stelios Ramfos in *O Kaimos tou Enos*, 42–51.

---

person is not some abstract philosophical entity. It is "the bio-historical nature deified in Christ." Panagopoulos rejects the idea of absolute otherness. He also rejects the definition of the person as relation. Relation does not pre-exist the person but follows it. Our deified human nature is connected with *sanctification*; it is not defined by ecstatic love.

Other writers since Panagopoulos have continued to question these ideas. In 2002 Lucian Turcescu argued against the distinction between the individual and the person.[53] He maintained that the Cappadocians, to whom Zizioulas appeals for his interpretation of the person, understand the person in terms of the individual. Aristotle Papanikolaou, while supporting Zizioulas, remarks that he "almost completely neglects that particular, ascetical struggle of a person in their particular relationship with God."[54] His over-all judgment is: "If the core of Christian faith is communion with God the Father, in the person of Christ, by the power of the Holy Spirit, it is difficult to think how such a communion does not imply an ontology that is relational and personal."[55]

The fullest response to Yannaras and Zizioulas on these issues has come from the religious philosopher, Stelios Ramfos.[56] Whilst

---

[53]L. Turcescu, " 'Person' versus 'Individual', and Other Modern Misreadings of Gregory of Nyssa," *Modern Theology* 18 (2002), 97–109. Turcescu has been ably answered by Aristotle Papanikolaou, "Is John Zizioulas an Existentialist in Disguise? Response to Lucian Turcescu," *Modern Theology* 20 (2004), 587–593.

[54]Papanikolaou, *Being With God*, 125.

[55]Ibid., 161.

[56]Ramfos, *O Kaimos tou Enos*. An English translation is forthcoming from Holy Cross Orthodox Press.

acknowledging the cogency of their arguments, he is not convinced that Yannaras's espousal of the hesychast tradition answers modern needs. Nor is he persuaded by either Yannaras or Zizioulas that personhood resides in relation. To make relation the bearer of personhood seems to him to diminish inwardness, interiority and subjective feeling. How can we speak of the kingdom "within us," as Yannaras does, if we are not primarily individuals? As for Zizioulas, Ramfos believes that he passes too easily from the divine Persons, distinguished only by relation, to the human person as a biological unit. Zizioulas consequently makes personal existence depend on sacramental symbolism. His idea of the person, in Ramfos's view, does not do justice to the fact that personhood is not simply a theological construct but has an anthropological basis. We have still not developed an adequate Christian anthropology.

As his own contribution to an anthropological as distinct from a theological perspective, Ramfos proposes the revival of an idea first put forward in the sixth century by Leontius of Byzantium. This is the idea of *enhypostasia*. When one thing is "enhypostasized" in another, it goes beyond its natural boundaries, taking on the characteristics of what enhypostasizes it and thus creating a third reality. Leontius's example is that of the wick and flame that make a torch: "For the wick is one thing and the fiery essence of the flame is another, but being *with* each other and *in* each other they both make a single torch." The person, in Ramfos's view is like the flame of the torch, which before being lit corresponds to the natural human being, a closed individual self. The light which "enhypostasizes" the "I" of my individuality is what constitutes the person. The person transcends the self, so that the person "cannot be identified wholly with the ego or be submerged in the group aspect of social relationship."[57] What makes me a person is my immanent and at the same time transcendent self—an interior otherness which is different from the ego.

What is important for Ramfos is the ability of the self to stand back and observe itself—its reflexiveness. He is convinced that we need to become *individuals* first in order to become persons. We have to learn not to take our identity from the group. We cannot attain union with God until we first become unified within ourselves. An identity that derives from the group and relies on symbolic forms prevents us from becoming our authentic selves. In recent years the debate about the *person* has been fundamental to any talk about union with God. If we are to unite with God we have to know where we are starting from, what it is we are trying to unite with God. We are not just relations. Nor are we just individual points of consciousness. Our identity resides in the fact that we are reflexive embodied beings who attain union with God by the expenditure of self and by freedom with respect to self. This is what self-transcendence means.

[57]Ibid., 346.

epilogue
DO YOU LIVE IT?

When my book on theosis in the Greek Fathers was published a few years ago, I showed a copy to a Jewish friend, a student of the Kabbala. He looked through it intently for some minutes, then said, "Yes, but do you live it?" A humbling question. Theosis is not just a subject of study. If it does not affect us personally, if it does not become the context in which we lead our Christian lives, it has no more value than any other topic of intellectual curiosity.

In this book we have met some of the great spiritual fathers of recent times who have been seen transfigured with light or have written about their own mystical experience. But as Metropolitan John Zizioulas has said, mystical experience is not to be identified solely with the extraordinary and unusual. The fact that theosis encompasses the whole of the economy of salvation means that it is intended for all believers without exception. To live theosis, then, means to lead our life in an eschatological perspective within the ecclesial community, striving through prayer, participation in the Eucharist, and the practice of the moral life to attain the divine likeness, being conformed spiritually and corporeally to the body of Christ until we are brought into Christ's identity and arrive ultimately at union with the Father. In simpler terms, it means for an Orthodox Christian to live as a faithful member of the Church, attending the Liturgy, receiving the sacraments and keeping the commandments. Nothing more—or less—than that.

The spirituality of the Orthodox Church is both liturgical and monastic. Liturgical spirituality takes full account of our corporeal nature. For the body is part of our identity. It is not something to be ignored or despised. The annual cycle of Great Feasts, particularly the Nativity, the Theophany, the Resurrection, the Ascension and the Transfiguration of Christ celebrate the transformation of humanity, body and soul, and its exaltation to heaven. On Holy Cross Day "the whole creation is set free from corruption.[1] On Christmas Day "has God come upon earth, and man gone up to heaven."[2] On the Forefeast of the Theophany Christ "opens the heavens, brings down the divine Spirit, and grants man a share of incorruption."[3] On the Feast of the Transfiguration Christ "has changed the darkened nature of Adam, and filling it with brightness He has made it godlike."[4] These feasts do not simply commemorate past events. With their eschatological dimension, frequently reinforced by the present tense of the verbs, they turn the worshiper "towards the future—towards the 'splendor of the Resurrection' at the Last Day, towards the 'beauty of the divine Kingdom' which all Christians hope eventually to enjoy."[5]

[1]*Festal Menaion* (Trans. Mother Mary and Archimandrite Kallistos Ware), 139.

[2]Ibid., 263.

[3]Ibid., 301.

[4]Ibid., 469.

[5]Ibid., 63.

Monastic spirituality is not separate from the Liturgy but an outgrowth from it. It has been nourished historically by the *Philokalia* and the way of hesychastic prayer. In the chapters on the Transfiguration and the Christian's passage from the image to the likeness of God we have looked at the testimonies of a number of monastic teachers. Theosis for them is an ascetical spiritual journey that culminates in the vision of God. Writers whose works are illuminating on this aspect of deification include Vladimir Lossky, Andreas Andreopoulos, Father Dumitru Stăniloae, Archimandrite Vasileios (Gontikakis) and Metropolitan Kallistos (Ware). One does not have to be a monk to profit from their works.

Another Orthodox approach has centered on speculation on the nature of the human person. Here the debate is lively and there are different points of view. One dividing line is between those who regard the essence-energies distinction as important and those who do not. Christos Yannaras is the leading representative of the great majority who do regard it as absolutely crucial. For him it is the energies that make God accessible to us and enable us to share in the divine life. Without our participation in the energies, God would remain inaccessible to us in his utter transcendence. Metropolitan John Zizioulas, on the other hand, wants to play down the importance of the energies. For him it is communion with the incarnate Word that enables us to share in the life of God. On the energies issue he is followed cautiously by Aristotle Papanikolaou. Father John Behr, with his focus on the mystery of Christ, also seems sympathetic to this approach.

Another dividing line separates those who identify personhood with *relation* from those who locate it in the *individual*. On this issue Yannaras and Zizioulas are both on the same side. Our personhood is constituted by our reaching out to the "other," and ultimately to the "Other," who is God. This reaching out is expressed by the categories of eros and ecstasy. Without it we are condemned to existential loneliness. A different point of view has been put by Stelios Ramfos: "Before any relation with a fellow human being, the 'other' exists inside me as a transcendent self." What we need in order to realize our personhood, in Ramfos's view, is not so much to go out of ourselves in ecstasy as to go into ourselves more deeply. We need to develop our interiority before we can reach out to find fulfillment in God.

These approaches are in the end convergent, not contradictory—although there are disagreements. This is often how modern reflections work to receive and convey the patristic witness. The faith of the Fathers is never superseded; it keeps us firmly anchored to the normative experience of the Church. But modern theologians do help us to reflect on it. Father Andrew Louth has made a useful distinction between historical theology as revitalizing the *memory* of the Church, and speculative theology as cultivating a genuinely critical *intelligence*.[6] The fact that modern theologians disagree in the exercise of their critical intelligence does not undermine the Church's memory, the witness of the Fathers. St Gregory Palamas sets us an example in this regard. In his sermons to the people of Thessalonica, whose bishop he became in 1347, he teaches them that we are rewarded and deified in our inner being through participating in the Church's fasts and vigils, in virtue of Christ's sharing in our human mortality. It is only in his controversial writings,

---

[6]Andrew Louth, "Is Development of Doctrine a Valid Category for Orthodox Theology?" In V. Hotchkiss and P. Henry, eds., *Orthodoxy and Western Culture: A Collection of Essays Honoring Jaroslav Pelikan on His Eightieth Birthday* (Crestwood, NY: St Vladimir's Seminary Press, 2005), 45–63.

when he is addressing his fellow intellectuals, that he develops the philosophical and theological basis for the essence-energies distinction.[7] He did not allow the speculative side of his thinking to confuse the ordinary believer. Those who found it helpful to use his thinking were free to do so, and the mid-fourteenth century synods of Constantinople pronounced it Orthodox. Other approaches, however, could coexist with it provided they did not attack it. Like St Gregory, modern thinkers today can help us deepen our appreciation of the patristic witness by approaching theosis from a variety of different angles.

Finally, the intense interest shown in theosis in recent years by non-Orthodox theologians should also be noted.[8] Lutherans, in particular, have studied the notion of theosis closely to see how it can enrich their ideas of sanctification and justification. This is to be welcomed. If theosis is a fundamental human right, as Archbishop Anastasios (Yannoulatos) has suggested, it cannot remain the exclusive possession of the Orthodox. Yet it is only within the Orthodox perspective—the Orthodox understanding of the

[7]For a discussion see my article "Theosis and Gregory Palamas: Continuity or Doctrinal Change?" *SVTQ* 50/4 (2006), 357–379.

[8]Publications include a book by a Finnish Lutheran author, Veli-Matti Kärkkäinen, *One With God: Salvation as Deification and Justification* (Collegeville, MN: Liturgical Press, 2004); the two books already mentioned issuing from Drew University, a Methodist foundation (see p. 19, note 9); and a lucid exposition of patristic teaching by a Roman Catholic author, Daniel A. Keating, *Deification and Grace* (Naples, FL: Sapientia, 2007). Father Andrew Louth has drawn my attention also to a new interest in sophiology by the Western 'radical orthodoxy' movement. See Brandon Gallaher, "Graced Creatureliness: Ontological Tension in the Uncreated/Created Distinction in the Sophiologies of Solov'ev, Bulgakov and Milbank," *Logos: A Journal of Eastern Christian Studies* 47 (2006), 163–90.

divine economy—that theosis acquires its full theological, spiritual and ecclesial dimensions. The Bible and the Fathers continue to engage with Orthodox theologians/philosophers, provoking new thinking. The debates which began with Bulgakov, Berdyaev and Lossky and have been carried forward by Yannaras, Zizioulas and Ramfos have not yet reached their conclusion. Further Orthodox thinking on theosis will no doubt explore more fully its anthropological and ecclesial aspects. On these aspects the Fathers have laid the foundations but have not pronounced the last word. Work still needs to be done on the Orthodox understanding of the nature of the human person and the nature of the Church. Central to this work will be an appreciation of the multi-faceted character of theosis.

bibliography & further reading

Alfeyev, Hilarion. *St Symeon the New Theologian and Orthodox Tradition*. Oxford: Oxford University Press, 2000.

Anatolios, Khaled. *Athanasius: The Coherence of His Thought*. London/New York: Routledge, 1998.

Andreopoulos, Andreas. *Metamorphosis: The Transfiguration in Byzantine Theology and Iconography*. Crestwood, NY: St Vladimir's Seminary Press, 2005.

Balfour, David. *Saint Gregory the Sinaite: Discourse on the Transfiguration*. Athens: Offprint from *Theologia* (1981/83) 1982.

Bartos, Emil. *Deification in Eastern Orthodox Theology: An Evaluation and Critique of the Theology of Dumitru Stăniloae*. Carlisle, Cumbria: Paternoster Press, 1999.

Behr, John. *The Mystery of Christ: Life in Death*. Crestwood, NY: St Vladimir's Seminary Press, 2006.

Berdyaev, Nicolas. *Slavery and Freedom*. R. M. French, trans. London: Geoffrey Bles, 1943.

———. *Spirit and Reality*. George Reavey, trans. London: Geoffrey Bles, 1939.

———. *The Beginning and the End*. R. M. French, trans. London: Geoffrey Bles, 1952.

———. *The Destiny of Man*. Natalie Duddington, trans. 2nd edn. London: Geoffrey Bles, 1945.

Bradshaw, David. *Aristotle East and West: Metaphysics and the Division of Christendom.* Cambridge: Cambridge University Press, 2004.

Bulgakov, Sergius. *The Bride of the Lamb.* Boris Jakim, trans. Grand Rapids, Michigan: Eerdmans/Edinburgh: T&T Clark, 2002.

————.*The Comforter.* Boris Jakim, trans. Grand Rapids, Michigan: Eerdmans, 2004.

————. *The Lamb of God.* Boris Jakim, trans. Grand Rapids, Michigan: Eerdmans, 2007.

Chrestou, Panagiotes K. *Partakers of God.* Brookline, MA: Holy Cross Orthodox Press, 1984.

Christensen, Michael J. and Wittung, Jeffery A., eds. *Partakers of the Divine Nature: The History and Development of Deification in the Christian Traditions.* Madison/Teaneck: Fairleigh Dickinson University Press, 2007

Chryssavgis, John. *Ascent to Heaven: The Theology of the Human Person according to Saint John of the Ladder.* Brookline, MA: Holy Cross Orthodox Press, 1989.

Cooper, Adam G. *The Body in St Maximus the Confessor: Holy Flesh, Wholly Deified.* Oxford: Oxford University Press, 2005.

Copleston, Frederick C. *Russian Religious Philosophy: Selected Aspects.* Tunbridge Wells, Kent: Search Press/Notre Dame, Indiana: University of Notre Dame Press, 1988.

Evdokimov, Paul. *L'Orthodoxie.* Neuchâtel, Switzerland: Éditions Dalechaux et Niestlé, 1965.

Finch, Jeffrey D. "Neo-Palamism, Divinizing Grace, and the Breach between East and West." In Michael J. Christensen and Jeffery A. Wittung, eds. *Partakers of the Divine Nature.* Madison/Teaneck: Fairleigh Dickinson University Press, 2007, 233–249.

Finlan, Stephen. "The Comedy of Divinization in Soloviev." In Stephen Finlan and Vladimir Kharlamov, eds. *Theōsis: Deification in Christian Theology.* Eugene, Oregon: Pickwick Publications, 2006, 168–183.

Gustafson, Richard F. "Soloviev's Doctrine of Salvation." In J. D. Kornblatt and R. F. Gustafson, eds., *Russian Religious Thought*. Madison, WI: University of Wisconsin Press, 1996, 31–48.

Hallonsten, Gösta. "*Theosis* in Recent Research: A Renewal of Interest and a Need for Clarity." In Michael J. Christensen and Jeffery A. Wittung, eds. *Partakers of the Divine Nature*. Madison/Teaneck: Fairleigh Dickinson University Press, 2007, 281–293.

Harakas, Stanley S. *Toward Transfigured Life: The* Theoria *of Eastern Orthodox Ethics*. Minneapolis, Minnesota: Light and Life Publishing Co., 1983.

Harrison, Nonna Verna. "Theosis as Salvation: An Orthodox Perspective." *Pro Ecclesia* 6 (1997), 429–443.

Jakim, Boris. "Sergius Bulgakov: Russian *Theosis*." In Michael J. Christensen and Jeffrey A. Wittung, eds. *Partakers of the Divine Nature*. Madison/Teaneck: Fairleigh Dickinson University Press, 2007, 250–259.

Keating, Daniel A. *The Appropriation of Divine Life in Cyril of Alexandria*. Oxford: Oxford University Press, 2004.

Lossky, Vladimir. *In the Image and Likeness of God*. John H. Erickson and Thomas E. Bird, eds. Crestwood, NY: St Vladimir's Seminary Press, 1974.

———. *The Mystical Theology of the Eastern Church*. Crestwood, NY: St Vladimir's Seminary Press, 1976.

———. *The Vision of God*. Asheleigh Moorhouse, trans. Crestwood, NY: St Vladimir's Seminary Press, 1976 (1963).

Louth, Andrew. *The Origins of the Christian Mystical Tradition*. Oxford: Oxford University Press, 1981. (2nd edn 2007).

———. "The Place of *Theosis* in Orthodox Theology." In Michael J. Christensen and Jeffery A. Wittung, eds. *Partakers of the Divine Nature*. Madison/Teaneck: Fairleigh Dickinson University Press, 2007, 32–44.

McGuckin, John Anthony. *The Transfiguration of Christ in Scripture and Tradition*. Lewiston/Queenston: Edwin Mellen Press, 1986.

————. The Strategic Adaptation of Deification in the Cappadocians." In Michael J. Christensen and Jeffery A. Wittung, eds. *Partakers of the Divine Nature*. Madison/Teaneck: Fairleigh Dickinson University Press, 2007, 95–114.

Mantzaridis, Georgios. *The Deification of Man: St Gregory Palamas and the Orthodox Tradition*. Liadain Sherrard, trans. Crestwood, NY: St Vladimir's Seminary Press, 1984.

Meyendorff, John. *A Study of St Gregory Palamas*. Leighton Buzzard, Bedfordshire: Faith Press, 1964.

————. "Theosis in the Eastern Christian Tradition." In Louis Dupré and Don E. Saliers, eds. *Christian Spirituality: Post-Reformation and Modern*. New York: Crossroad, 1989, 470–476.

Moutsoulas, Elias D. *The Incarnation of the Word and the Theosis of Man according to the Teaching of Gregory of Nyssa*. Constantine J. Andrews, trans. Athens, 2000.

Nellas, Panayiotis. *Deification in Christ: Orthodox Perspectives on the Nature of the Human Person*. Norman Russell, trans. Crestwood, NY: St Vladimir's Seminary Press, 1987.

Papanikolaou, Aristotle. *Being With God: Trinity, Apophaticism, and Divine-Human Communion*. Notre Dame, Indiana: University of Notre Dame Press, 2006.

The Philokalia. The Complete Text compiled by St Nikodemos of the Holy Mountain and St Makarios of Corinth. G. E. H. Palmer, Philip Sherrard and Kallistos Ware, eds. and trans. 4 vols to date. London: Faber and Faber, 1979 ff.

Ramsey, Arthur Michael. *The Glory of God and the Transfiguration of Christ*. London: Longman Green, 1949.

Ramfos, Stelios. *Like a Pelican in the Wilderness: Reflections on the sayings of the Desert Fathers*. Norman Russell, trans. Brookline, MA: Holy Cross Orthodox Press, 2000.

————. *O Kaimos tou Enos*. Athens: Armos, 2000 (English trans. by Norman Russell forthcoming from Holy Cross Orthodox Press).

Russell, Norman. *The Doctrine of Deification in the Greek Patristic Tradition*. Oxford: Oxford University Press, 2004.

————. " 'Partakers of the Divine Nature' (2 Peter 1:4) in the Byzantine Tradition." In J. Chrysostomides, ed., *Kathegetria: Essays Presented to Joan Hussey on her 80th Birthday*. Camberley: Porphyrogenitus, 1988, 51–67.

————. "Theosis and Gregory Palamas: Continuity or Doctrinal Change?" *SVTQ* 50/4 (2006), 357–379.

Solovyev, Vladimir. *Lectures on Godmanhood*. Peter Zouboff, trans. London: Dennis Dobson, 1948. (A revised edition by Boris Jakim has been published under the title *Lectures on Divine Humanity*. Hudson, NY: Lindisfarne, 1995.)

Sophrony (Sakharov), Archimandrite. *St Silouan the Athonite*. Crestwood, NY: St Vladimir's Seminary Press, 1999. (Originally published in 1991 by the Patriarchal Stavropegic Monastery of St John the Baptist, Tolleshunt Knights by Maldon, Essex, adapted in turn from *The Undistorted Image: Staretz Silouan: 1866–1938*. Rosemary Edmonds, trans. London: Faith Press, 1958.)

————. *We Shall See Him As He Is*. Rosemary Edmonds, trans. Tolleshunt Knights, Essex: Stavropegic Monastery of St. John the Baptist, 1988.

Stăniloae, Dumitru. *The Experience of God*. Ioan Ionita and Robert Barringer ed. and trans. vol. i, *Revelation and Knowledge of the Triune God*; vol. ii, *The Word: Creation and Deification*. Brookline, MA: Holy Cross Orthodox Press, 1994 and 2000.

————. *Orthodox Spirituality*. Archim. Jerome (Newville) and Otilia Kloos, trans. South Canaan, PA: St. Tikhon's Seminary Press, 2002.

Stavropoulos, Archimandrite Christoforos. *Partakers of the Divine Nature*. Stanley Harakas, trans. Minneapolis, Minnesota: Light and Life Publishing Co., 1976.

Swoboda, Philip J. " 'Spiritual Life' versus Life in Christ. S. L. Frank and the Patristic Doctrine of Deification." In J. D. Kornblatt and

R. F. Gustafson, eds, *Russian Religious Thought*. Madison WI: University of Wisconsin Press, 1996, 234–248.

Thomas, Stephen. *Deification in the Eastern Orthodox Tradition: A Biblical Perspective*. Piscataway, NJ: Gorgias Press, 2007.

Vasileios, Archimandrite. *Hymn of Entry: Liturgy and Life in the Orthodox Church*. Elizabeth Brière, trans. Crestwood, NY: St Vladimir's Seminary Press, 1984.

Ware, Metropolitan Kallistos. "Deification in St Symeon the New Theologian." *Sobornost incorporating Eastern Churches Review* 25.2 (2003), 7–29.

————. "Salvation and Theosis in Orthodox Theology." In *Luther et la réforme allemande dans une perspective oecuménique*. W. Schneemelcher, ed. Geneva: Editions du Centre Orthodoxe, 1983, 167–184.

————. *The Inner Unity of the Philokalia and its Influence in East and West*. Athens: Alexander S. Onassis Foundation, 2004.

Wesche, Kenneth Warren. "Eastern Orthodox Spirituality: Union with God in *Theosis*." *Theology Today* 56 (1999), 29–43.

Winslow, Donald F. *The Dynamics of Salvation: A Study in Gregory of Nazianzus*. Philadelphia, PA: Philadelphia Patristic Foundation, 1979.

Yannaras, Christos. *Elements of Faith: An Introduction to Orthodox Theology*. Keith Schram, trans. Edinburgh: T&T Clark, 1991.

————. *On the Absence and Unknowability of God: Heidegger and the Areopagite*. Andrew Louth, ed. Haralambos Ventis, trans. London/New York: T&T Clark International, 2005.

————. *Person and Eros*. Norman Russell, trans. Brookline, MA: Holy Cross Orthodox Press, 2007.

————. *The Freedom of Morality*. Elizabeth Brière, trans. Crestwood, NY: St Vladimir's Seminary Press, 1984.

————. *Variations on the Song of Songs*. Norman Russell, trans. Brookline, MA: Holy Cross Orthodox Press, 2005.

Yannoulatos, Archbishop Anastasios. *Facing the World: Orthodox*

Essays on Global Concerns. Pavlos Gottfried, trans. Crestwood, New York: St Vladimir's Seminary Press, 2003.

Zizioulas, John D. *Being as Communion: Studies in Personhood and the Church.* Crestwood, NY: St Vladimir's Seminary Press, 1985.

———. *Communion and Otherness: Further Studies in Person-hood and the Church.* Paul McPartlan, ed. London: T&T Clark, 2006.

index

the author

Norman Russell is an independent scholar who has written widely on Orthodox themes, specializing in early Greek patristics and fourteenth-century hesychasm. He is the author of *The Doctrine of Deification in the Greek Patristic Tradition.*